THE DIABOLICAL DICTIONARY OF MODERN ENGLISH

It's the most irreverent assay of the *lingua franca* since Ambrose Bierce's **DEVIL'S DICTIONARY**, a roguish, acerbic counterattack against modern mores and pretentions of every stripe.

From Birth Control, n. (a method of avoiding the issue), to Venom, n. (the ink of scorn), R.W. Jackson tears into the body politic—and cultural—with sharp wit and ready riposte, leaving no tern unstoned and no windbag aloft.

Join the fun with the dictionary that tells the wicked truth about the language we use—and the tongue that uses us!

THE IRREVERENT REFERENCE

Brain-dead, adj. Alive and well. Viable. Plugged in. Concerned. Aware.

Carcinogen, n. An agent that causes rats to chew gum rather than smoke cigarettes.

Cro-Magnon, adj. Relating to a species of pre-Beaujolais Frenchmen.

Hairpiece, n. A wig worn by a bald man, giving the appearance of a bald man wearing a wig.

Health care, n. The necessary and humanitarian service provided by civilized societies to rich and poor alike. The taxpayer is left to fend for himself.

Levite, n. One who wears jeans religiously.

From Washington to L.A. from East Coast chic to West Coast cool, from sex, sin, and politics to the media and more, here's the ultimate irreverent reference from R. W. Jackson, spiritual heir of Jonathan Swift, Samuel Johnson, and Ambrose Bierce, and author of . . .

The Diabolical Dictionary
of Modern English

QUANTITY SALES

INDIVIDUAL SALES

THE

DIABOLICAL
DICTIONARY
OF
MODERN
ENGLISH

COMPLETE AND UNBRIDLED

R. W. JACKSON

To Fortuity
and also to the memory of the
great Ambrose Bierce

A LAUREL BOOK
Published by
Dell Publishing
a division of
Bantam Doubleday Dell Publishing Group, Inc.
666 Fifth Avenue
New York, New York 10103

ISBN: 0-440-20591-3

Reprinted by arrangement with Delacorte Press

Printed in the United States of America

Published simultaneously in Canada

One Previous Dell Edition

New Laurel Edition

May 1990

10 9 8 7 6 5 4 3 2 1

OPM

Acknowledgment

Special thanks (and a cigar or two) to Mr. Jon Crawford for his helpful suggestions in the preparation of the final manuscript of this estimable dictionary.

Contents

Abbreviations That May Be Used In This Work

a	CIO	Fud.
A	CIPAYLATE	G.A.W.K.
a.	CITRIK	GermWar
A.	comp.	GeRMweet.
aa	con	gErmJunQ.
AA	corn.	Gr.A.B.
a.a.	Crapp.	HANG.
A.A.	Cym.	Inc.
AAA	czechoslovakia	Jupe
A.A.A.	Da.-da	Kann.
AAAA	DdS	LamE
A.A.A.A.	Dim.	NOs.
AAAAA	Dum.	O.D.
A.A.A.A.A.	eA	prOst
A.A.A.A.L.	E.T.Z.A.J.R.K.	q.v.
A.A.A.F.	EZMUNE	Rev.
A.A.S.	ezzgml	S.L.A.N.T.
A.B.	ezzgmoe	tLt
abbrev.	F.	UL.t.
Abus.	FedCon.	Vaan
Abyss.	FedRook	Whoor
Ataxi.	FedSquand.	XL
Bab.	FibFed.	Yak.
Bang.	FlamFed	z
Beng.	FlimFed.	Z
Bong.	FRAck	z.
Bung.	FRIS	Z.
c.	FriZZ	zz

ZZ	Z.Z.Z.	Z.Z.Z.Z.
Z.z	ZZZZ	ZZZZZZ
Z.Z.	Z.Z.Z.Z.	Z.Z.Z.Z.Z.Z.
ZZ	ZZZZZ	Z.Z.Z.ZZZ_zzzzzzzzz

Preface

This dictionary is a totally new work, containing well over twenty-eight entries, and is intended for the modern and discerning reader who is interested in keeping abreast of current and proper usage. It includes most of the new and pertinent medical and technical terms as well as the literary and politico-celebrital, embracing only such slang English as deemed tasteful by the editors. The definitions of "acronym," "acupuncture," "junk food," "Central America," and "sports medicine" will be seen to be particularly useful to connoisseur and layman alike, and are treated with inordinate concern. Except that the work tends occasionally to lapse into a singular and unaccountable inventiveness, adopting a fervor of unorthodoxy and attention to stylistic detail heretofore rare in the medium, and thought by some experts to be cavalier and unnecessary to its intent to inform, the general tone sought for the dictionary is one of popular eclecticism, a posture urged by linguistic surveyors, market analysts, and university curriculogians of no mean credential, the world over.

Certain lexicographical illustrations and verse are also included in this tome, not to unscholarlylike embellish it but to disestablish the kind of stuffiness and tedium inherent in the reading of some inferior dictionaries, especially the kind that calls itself "comic." Some entries are appended by the names of their contributors, a practice not unprecedented in word-bookery and to which the distinguished editors of this notable volume respectfully subscribe.

Grateful appreciation is extended to the renowned sousier, Chef Robbere, whose name frequently appears in these pages due to the current enormous popularity of restauranting, gourmet dining, and other fast-food consumption, and without whose dry astuteness and herby panhandiness many important parts of this excellent guide would not have been possible.

Canto Blissfield
EDITOR IN CHIEF

(Master)
(Boss)
(Sir)
Madame, shall I begin with the usual jokes?
—ARISTOPHANES

Suggestion to the User

The greatest appreciation of this superior reference
will be gained by reading it in the morning, on an
empty stomach, or half an hour after consuming a
light breakfast and a couple of cigarettes.

R.W.J.

a

A *n* The first letter of the American alphabet soup. A borrowing of the English *alkies* or the Greek *alpha,* meaning "a beginning from which the remainder deteriorates." It is also the front, low-brow vowel of "rat," "trash," "scam," "graft," etc., a two-syllable feminine suburban vowel which is pronounced "éa," as in "bléab," "shéack," "néag," "réash," etc.

Abbreviation *n* A grammatical diminution wherein the important part of a word remains and a symbol replaces the rest, as in
Wishing you a Xy Xmas & a Xpy Xyear
SCRAWLMARK CARDS

Abiogenesis *n* The production of a living organism from lifeless matter, as in God's creation of the cynic from the formless void of condos.

Adjective *n* A part of speech invented by the Over-the-Counter school of grammar, combining the best part of an adjective with the aberrances of an ad-man.
The *clean* is better with Frag soap.
You get more *dry* with Pitesque.

Your *cool* is bigger with Dyspepsi Cola.

BILL BLAST

Ablution *n*   The sanitizing of a worshiper prior to the day's misdeeds. A few select believers, however, give greater consideration to the higher spiritual cleansings, and can be seen each morning raising the consciousness with an eye-opener as soon as the corner baptismals open for business.

Abound *vi*   To exist most plentifully.

Abounder *n*   One who exists most plentifully.

Absinthe   A meaningless catchword invented by a wise man, and by which a blockhead irresistibly urges his identity.

> "Absinthe" leads the fool to ponder
>   A quick and easy line to pass,
> As "Absinthe makes the tart responder"
>   Or some such awful gas.

SEXTUS DUNDERUS IMPROPRIETUS

Absolute zero   The prospect of magnanimity, on a scale of 1 to 273.

Abstract art   The product of the poverty-stricken artist who can never afford any art.

S. THETIK

Acapulco *n*   A suburb of Orange County, in the Lesser Tortillas. Formerly a Grayline protectorate, Acapulco was annexed by Wurst Western Inc. in 1958, at the Battle of Cardboard Walls, with an assault led by General Francisco-Franchise against the corrupt Santa Anita. It is said that sleepless and dyspeptic *turistas* then charged upon the streets and could be heard shouting "Remember the à la mode" to thieving waiters, as their luggage was dragged off, never to be heard from again. Testimony of former prisoners of a Hyatt, in Cozumel, revealed similar atrocities.

Achieve *vt* To get a heart attack before a liberal arts grad.

Acronym *n* A word-abbreviation, as Society of Liberals and Opinion Pollsters, or Center for Rehabilitation of American Prisoners. It is usually kept to four letters, although shorter ones, such as Association of Satanists and Suburbanites, or Men of Brains, and longer, General Retail Enterprises and Economic Development, do occasionally appear.

Activism *n* Supremacy of the mouth over matters of the mind-less.

Acupuncture *n* The puncturing of a purse prior to the needling of a ninny.

Adjusted *adj* Said of imbeciles and illiterates, that is, collegians, or those to whom grammar is repugnant and smiling is natural. *Syn* Californian.

Admonish *vt* To encourage children by telling them not to go with strangers, because criminals have rights, police are impotent, people are vicious, trust is foolhardy, judges are capricious, law is subverted, justice is a sham, integrity is folly, lawyers are scavengers, prosecutors are incompetent, juries are tampered with, citizens are apathetic, accountability is extinct, and prisons are overcrowded.

HUGO NAWT

Adverb *n* An extinct modifier unnecessary to success in the Age of Jockism, 1977–present.

ANNA PEST

"It's a good idea to eat light."

CHIP & DEBBIE SUNNYE

Advice *n* Any dispensation of misinformation inducing a sense of worthiness in oneself and abjection in another.

Aerobics *n* A humiliation similar to exercise but not as smelly.

Affair *n* An extravenerital disappointment that serves to strengthen the bond of alimony. Prior to the Christian Era affairs were called "cheating."

NOAH PHALT

Afferent *adj* Of the nerve fibers that carry messages to the brain—as distinguished from **affronts**, which carry all messages from the brain.

BERTRAND TUSSLE

Affirmative action Socialist chopped liver prepared by force-feeding the Republican goose.

Afterthought *n* Reason.

"As only the higher brutes, capable of after-thoughts."

QUIVERSPEARE

Age of majority   Incipient cupidity.

Aggressive *adj*   Preeminent in abusing the wisdom of sloth.

Ain't   The contraction of *ain not,* from the language of the savage tribe of Aine, of Oolong-Pootong, the members of which society are commonly referred to as Ainuses. The contraction has no meaning, and Ainuses use it when they do not intend to say anything, or when they do.

Al dente *adj*   One of four ways in which food is over-cooked at a gourmet restaurant.

CHEF ROBBERE

Alias *n*   A drab imposture assumed by crooks. For example:
   Persia, AKA Iran, or Itoldyahowmany
   Constantinople, AKA Instantbul
   Siam, AKA Thighland
   St. Petersburg, AKA Leningrab
   Serbia, AKA Yougoslave

STRABO MERCATOR

Alien *n*   An unholy being, having descended from the heavens in a fiery vehicle, and demanding tribute and obedience to its commands, the alternative being an infernal retribution.

Aliorelative *n* A philosophical term implying diversity if not related to itself or denied by the reciprocal of its predicate. Compare
    Aliarelative: a real estate agent who is your brother-in-law
    Aleechrelative: a doctor in the family
    Alechrelative: an uncle
    Alienrelative: parent

ALFRED NORTH PIMPEL

Aloha *exclam* Pig latin for "Hello!"; *specif* "Hello, sucker!"

AM Ante Monotony. Also, in radio, Amply Moronic. Compare **FM**, Frequently Moronic.

BETELGEUSE JONES

AMBULANCE *n* AMBULANCE.

America *n* An equocracy whose principal industries are petroleum, cocaine, and briefcases.

DAISY WEAL

Analytic *adj* (L. *anal,* of the brain) Human thought. Compare
    Egolytic: human conversation
    Gallolytic: human commerce
    Biliolytic: human discussion
    Podialytic: human speech
    Spleenolytic: an editorial

EMMANUEL KAN

Anchor *n* A deadweight employed to keep a craft from going anywhere, or to prevent a derelict from drifting from channel to channel.

Android *n* A machine that looks like a director of development.

Announcer *n* A hollow tube through which signals are piped to the dead.

Answering machine A machine connected to a telephone. Answering machines are made in various sizes, but usually range from 4′10″ to 6′4″, and come in three or four ridiculous colors. Limited, hopelessly dull, and mechanical answers blare from them repeatedly, when rung up, and are, at best, garbled, predictable, obnoxious, hackneyed, witless, and mundane. Newer machines have *all* the answers.

RUDY MENTARRY

Ant *n* A cosmopolitan, antisocial insect of the order Hymnoterror that nests in deadwood (colonials) or is part of the underground (townhouses). Males and females for the most part are swarmers, especially when mating, and become annoyances to egghead ants, who sometimes enslave other species. The highest condition of an ant is called a pissmire, or beachfront. Ants are divided as follows:

Young Females	Extravag Ants and Impl Ants
Old Females	Termag Ants and Depress Ants
Young Males	Defend Ants, Arrog Ants

Old Males	Ped Ants, Tyr Ants
Mates	Galliv Ants
Professionals	Malign Ants and Flamboy Ants and Petul Ants
Media	Nuis Ants and Blat Ants
Politicos	Sycoph Ants and Redund Ants
Religios	C Ants, R Ants, Aberr Ants, and Vagr Ants
Taxpayers	Peas Ants
Military	GI Ants, Warr Ants
Minorities	Adam Ants, Conspir Ants
Noisemakers	Ten Ants, Occup Ants
Rock Concerts	Irrit Ants, Disson Ants
Celebrities	Indulg Ants, Inf Ants
Lexicographers	Sav Ants

ARTHUR O. PODDE

Anthropomorphism *n* The inflicting of human characteristics upon unsuspecting gods, demons, and animals.

Neither gods, beasts, nor demons rate
the prowess of His Highness, Man, to demonstrate.

CARDINAL SZINNE

Antipersonnel mine *n* An employment office.

Antiperspirant *n* A preparation used to keep the armpits dry while telling a lie.

Antique *n* An atrocity distinguished by age.

Anubis *n* An Egyptian god with the body of a clinical psychologist and the head of a jackal, who, scripture has it, will lead the dead to a bitter judgment. A striking comparison is the western god Wallstreet, whose body, however, is that of a barefoot pilgrim.

ANNA NIMMITEE

Apartheid *n* A horrendous social system of Africa. Compare **Togethertide,** a horrendous social system of America.

HARRY CRISHNA

Archimedean screw A device used to raise water, comprising a spiral tube, a shaft, and a cylinder revolved by an operator. As distinguished from **royal screw,** a machine used to raise revenue, consisting of a spiraling boob and a withholding tax, or a cylinder revolved into an operator.

Armageddon *n* The Final Battle, when the forces of Good will confront the Church, the jogger, the telephone, the sitcom, the Volvo, Martha's Vineyard, Halls of Fame, Sesame Street, Marcel Marceau, Countess Mara, whole-wheat bread, Motivation Seminars, and soccer.

GEORGE PAPAMAMADADACOPPAPLEEPOULOS

Arms talks A summit pertaining to the destruction of all life on earth, and the survival only of elementary particles, such as Swiss chocolatiers.

ADMIRAL BULL

Artificial insemination Unnatural—that is, erotic—impregnation.

Artistic *adj* Dead. *Ant* creative.

Assets *n* The hoardings and scrapings of an ass.

Assinine A word that is misspelled more appropriately than "knot."

Assist *vt* To increase the factor of incompetency by one.

Assizes *n* British seats of law. Official bodies whose domain is the privy, or court. In America assizes are Superior and Supreme.

Astrology *n* Divination based on the compunctions of the planets or the positions of a starlet, and the resultant influence upon human affairs. The influence of a heavenly body on a state legislator is said to be considerable.

LUCKY LUCY ONNO

Atheist *n* A popular infidel of questionable allegiance, though not a **theist.** According to Rabbi Hochbinder, a theist is one who believes that God is a chain motel-keeper and can be known by reservation—as distinguished from **deist,** one who avers that God is a slumlord and absentee owner and can be known by default. A **pantheist** is one who sees God in His works, essentially His mirrors.

DICK SHANERRY

Augury *n* The ancient science of predicting political trends by consulting the intestines of a sheep. Currently it is called the New Hampshire primary, and entails the gut-reaction of a jackass.

Automatic writing *n* The scrawl of necromancers and other charlatans such as ad-men, editorialists, and the reporters of news.

Available-light photography *n* Mortification of the flash.

Avuncular *adj* A word that, after wrestling a few syllables, says uncle. *Ant* **avauntular.**

Awareness *n* The prickly heat of a meddler.

Ax *vt* To propose a query, in a specialized urban environment. Retorts are hackneyed and incoherent.

b

Baby *n* In America, a blessing. In Mexico, something sold to an American.

MINNIE SEEREEZ

Backgammon *n* Checkers for the trendy. *Syn* tofu.

Back to Nature Said of humanity, which turned its back to Nature on March 9, 1852, at seven o'clock in the morning.

J. S. BACK

Backwards *adv* A favorite tack of the ship of state.

Ban *vt* To save the public morals by prohibiting corrupt, salacious, or pornographic materials and ideas that are unprofitable.

ANAL ROBERTS

Banana cream pie Currently, a round of yellow stuff topped with white stuff, which takes a lot of crust to serve. *Syn* coconut cream pie; homemade pastry.

CHEF ROBBERE

Bargain *n* Half off, allowing only a 70 percent profit margin. "Strike while the irony is hot."

HUGH A. DUBBYA

Basketball *n* A game played with five units on a side, and consisting of a superstar, an ultrasuperstar, a spectultrasuperstar, an epispectultrasuperstar, and a pentultepispectultrasuperstar. A superficial occasionally intercedes.

COACH ANPHOR

Battered child *n* One too young to misunderstand family life, or to buy a shotgun.

Battered husband *n* A wretch who brings home only half the pay that his fiancée expected.

Béarnaise *n* A sauce by which a prime beef is rendered palatable to a choice ass.

CHEF ROBBERE

Bed *n* Formerly an exclusive romantic vehicle, provided by nature, for the conception of chancres. Currently nature provides the pool table, the sleeping bag, the shower stall, the Jacuzzi, the flotation system, and the parking lot.

SIMON EISZ

Beech *n* In North America a species of nut-bearing tree. In South America a shrewish North American female.

Beef jerky Man. Compare **cheese jerky**, woman.

Beeper *n* A homing device sold with three-piece suits that allows them to find their way to offices of malpractice, malfeasance, and misrepresentation.

OXFORD WEENGTIPPE

Being *n* A state variously conceived and erroneously defined. The current improvement in the classic Cartesian pronouncement comes from Dr. Rex Humbug, prominent atavist, evangelist, and auto repossessor: "I think, therefore I scam." Other notable epistemological cogitations:

I think, therefore I sham: Fred Cartesian
I think, therefore I ham: W. Shakespeare
I think, therefore I aim: N. Bonaparte
I think, therefore I jam: Dizzy Gillespie

BARRY MANHOLE

Bestiality *n* Unknown in life, denounced in
death,
Tormented to the end;
I ask, thou Grim Activity,
Which are the beasts, which men!

THE OLD PHILOSOPHER

B girl *n* Best girl. An activist, with a larger circle of acquaintance.

Bible *n* The first eighty-one books of *The Wall Street Journal.* A volume of suggestive references thoughtfully provided by God for the titillation of sinners and the titlizations of other California filmmakers.

THE YOUNG LYIN'S TEND 'ER MERCIES

Bible Belt *n* Usually bonded bourbon, or white lightning (and brimstone).

Bibulous *adj* Not averse to a bibule, that is, an olive spiritually awash.

Big Dipper *n* A group of stars with the shape of a congressman.

Big shot *n* A misfire of low caliber, heard round the bored-room.

Big Toe *n* An accessory provided by nature to accommodate the coroner's tag.

JAWIN' DEAU

Bilingual *adj* Able to converse in two languages. Compare **trilingual**, able to converse in three languages; **cunilingual**, fluent in the universal language.

DEWEY URDOENTY

Biofeedback *n* Voluntary control of involuntary brute functions, as excretion, conversation, script reading, and acceptance speeches. Unpopular in America.

X. AWST

Bird of pray *n* A vulture commonly seen on its knees, feeding on the carrion of Will.

Birth *n* A trauma resulting in the debility of existence.

Birth control *n* A method of avoiding the issue.

Birth defect *n* Human procreation.

Bisexual *n* A participant, having been twice discouraged.

Black Friday A Friday. The fifth day of a colorless week.

ROY G. BIV

Black humor *n* An inexcusable irreverence for the indignity of death; examples of which opprobrious material the honorable editors of this eminently civilized volume decline to offer.

WHIT WALTMAN

Black tie *n* One unmistakable sign of a higher civilization. The others are the dead-bolt lock and pourable mustard.

KITTIE LYTTRE

Blair, Eric A shameful impostor who wrote a documentary about life in London in 1948, which seems to have deteriorated a bit since then.

Bleed *vt* A former practice of physicians and other leeches; currently employed by the Double Cross and Shield Company.

Blush *n* A cosmetic representing a mythical emotion of woman.

ANGIE O. PLASTIE

B Movie *n* Better movie. A California film improved in locations and verisimilitudes, and appealing to the majority of the viewing public; the A, or acro-cephalus, film being aimed at the elite. Both B and A movies are released with the following ratings to protect psyches:

G	Grunt
PG	Partial Grunt
R	Raspberry
X	Xenogenetic
Y	Yahoo
Z	Zzz...

FEDERICO OBSINI

Boca Raton *n* (Sp, mouths of rats) A Florida nest reserved for the rich.

Bodybuilder *n* One whose hobby has gone to his head. A major stockholder in mirrors and mineral oil. There are two kinds of bodybuilder: male and female. According to Prof. Del Toydz, Ph.D., a male bodybuilder is distinguishable from a female bodybuilder by the fact that the latter wears a smaller-size brassiere.

ARNOLD SWEATZENSWAGGERZ

Book *n* A mall novelty. There are two kinds of book: paperback and hardcore. The most popular of the hardcore are *The Guinness Book of World Absurds* and *Jane Conned a Workout*. All paperbacks are mushy dime novels by Isaac Asimuth.

Book of the Dead *n* The definitive history of Eastern and Western civilization.

Born-again *adj* Traumatized, at least twice.

Once is too much!

JACQUELINE SUESMANNE

Bourbon *n* An improvement of corn. Fire water. Royal water. Holy water.

> Noah brewed a hefty batch
> As soon as toady cracked the hatch.
> But first, enamored of the dry,
> He burnt his offering to the Sky,
> Uncertain of the earthy high.
> Tho, amid that fragrant crew, quite fond,
> Ne'er grog—St. Noah deserved a nip in bond!

RIP SNORTZ

Bowdlerize *vt* To remove tasteless passages from literature and put them on teevee, where they will be appreciated.

Brain-dead *adj* Alive and well. Viable. Plugged in. Concerned. Aware.

Brainwashing *n* A sanitizing and realigning of the political understanding after having been temporarily soiled by the dust of Principle or the grime of Ambition. Formerly, shrinkage occurred in the process, but the modern brain, treated by Medias, is, conveniently, preshrunk.

WES POYNTE

Bray *n* The supplication of a mule, which is always heard and occasionally answered—as opposed to **pray**, being the supplication of an ass, which is never heard and occasionally expensive.

Breakfast *n* A black ritual requiring the swallowing of the droppings of a chicken and the rash of a pig.

Bull *n* A Spanish animal of universal dimension, used for sport. In Spain the sport is called *bullfighting*, in England it is the defunct *bullbaiting*, and in North America the popular *bullthrowing*. The Spaniards use an ancient breed of bull called Andalusian, a sturdy animal which is first intimidated and then impaled, in an arena, by men in gaudy suits. The North Americans have developed increasingly hearty strains of bull, such as the implacable Conversasian, which can be somewhat intimidated but seldom impaled; the formidable Showbisian, which is endlessly thrown by noisy contestants dressed in awful sequined uniforms, at the California arenas; the invincible Pressian, a headstrong brute thrown the most often, in all areas of the continent; and the odious Politisian, which can be cowed only every two or four years. Ernest Hemmingwear's *Bullthrowing in the Afternoon* commemorates the first use of a Conversasian, which was impaled by a dry martini.

GALINDO HORNO

Burns, Robert A Scotsman who turned a speech impediment into poetry and a cigar label into glory.
> Tha' wee bit piece o' nibblin' cheese
> Doth vow auld sure-foot Death t' please,
> An cow'rin' beastie's soul to raise for evermore,
> Beyond ye frightful trapped maze and reason's roar.

O life thou art a galling load,
That a dishonest man's the noblest work o'
God;
And now is done, tho' na enuf today,
Of lords and princes gang aft and keelhauled
a-gley.

HIGHLAND HARRY

Business as usual   Service with a sneer.

C

Cabbage patch   A clump of dirt able to produce heads and cheap status-toys for adults. The latter is the more worthy of the two.

California *n*   New York warmed over.
MICKEY MOUTH

Camel hair   A coat plucked from one beast of foul disposition, and fitted to another.
TART, SHAFTSEM & PARKS

Canada *n*   A socialist protectorate full of nice people and clean streets, with no crime except teevee.

Capital punishment *n*   Antitrust.

Carcinogen *n*   An agent that causes rats to chew gum rather than smoke cigarettes.

Cardiac arrest *n*   The proper indictment and incarceration of a specialist.

Cardiologist *n*   A master of cards. A gambler who seldom loses.
> Twice told to lose weight
> And to increase the gait,
> To nip the cholesterol

And foul chemistry to pester all
Fat paunches. Hail boneyards!
'Twas not in the cards.

M. JUMBO

Career *n* The first day of a job.

Carob *n* A fodder sold in health-food stores, obtained from a tree and used for the cultivation of other saps. It is also utilized in fitness programs with dumbbells.

GAYLORD CONDEAU

Carport *n* An excellent Cockburn's '55, for the glove box.

Caste *n* Rigid classes based on social worth and principle, such as the Hindoo
Bramen: rulers and pornographers
Kashmen: criminals
Vicemen: real estate moguls
Suitmen: lawyers and statesmen
Untouched: the press
Touched: entertainers
Put-the-touch-on: sportsmen

MAHATMA DANDY

Caucasian *adj* From the Caucus. A race of fierce, warlike madmen from a region near Mt. Offen, in the Uranals. The tribe comprises Whites, Blacks, Tans, Drunks, Bunks, Skunks, Reds, Yellows, Pinkoes, Scotched-Plaids, and the awful clans of Hyannisport.

CAL A. FOREIGNYA

Causeless *adj* Having no basis in the existing body of guesswork. Of unknown or conjectural antecedents, as a politician or a celebrity.

Cavernous *adj* Deep and hollow in sound, as the blare of consultants, counselors, instructors, solicitors, professors, planners, designers, announcers, conferees, and the Eternal Order of Exasperating Expounders of Deecee.

BELLA KOSE

Cease-fire *n* A heavier reloading for an assault of stealth.

Censure *vt* To apprise a professional of the public's disgust with its impotence at redress.

Centaur *n* A monster with a man's head and arms, and the body and trunk of a Buick. According to legend, centaurs were the offspring of Exxon.

Central America An area rife with fanatic militarists, death squads, illicit drugs, assassins, refugees, rampant venereal disease, political unrest, and rigged elections, lying on an imaginary line extending west, at north latitude 38 degrees, from Washington, D.C., to San Francisco.

JOSE KANYUSZEE

Cess pool *n* A receptacle that receives drainage from a toilet. Compare **cess-Jacuzzi,** a receptacle that receives drainage from a Condo; **cess-mall,** a can that takes in dross from a parking lot; **cess-**

tennis, a dump placed near a cess pool for the drainage of a suburb.

BJORN BJESTERDAY

Champ *n* The masculine of "Princess." Also, *vt* & *vi* & *vd* to bite down, hard, when called that.

ED UHTORRYALIES

Chaperon *n* One who, at a noise function, sees to it that the teenage alcoholics do not light up a joint too brightly, or ask an adult for coke, before the fight in the parking lot.

CLEM BAYK

Chauvinism *n* An elegant economy founded by the eminent optopest, Prof. Thrombo Bleeg. It involves a devotion to patriotism, integrity, honor, men's rights, and other lost causes.

Cheap shot *n* Bar whiskey, neat, when bonded corn is anticipated.

Chiarobscuro *n* A tool of artists used to light a market while shading an ability at art.

Chicago *n* A midwest urb. According to California high-school students, Chicago is not Santa Monica and is possibly west of Rodeo Mall; but Indochina is not.

D. W. GRIFFTER

Chihuahua *n* A province of Mexico named in honor of a rat the size of a dog.

Childhood *n* A former condition of children prior to the Honesty Era, in North America, and the Human Rights Era, elsewhere. Currently the property of retirement communities.

ELLA VADER

Chile *n* Chili.

Chile con carne *n* Chili con carni.

Chili *n* Chile.

Chilli *n* Chile, Chili.

Chilli bean *n* An inhabitant of chili.

Chilli buff An insensitive brute who prefers spiced meat to salad bars, straight whiskey to cocktails, wit to humor, satire to drama, ports to sherries, discomfort to physicians, justice to lawyers, handball to racketball, opera to musicals, jazz to rock, and Henry Youngman to Robin Williams.

DUSTIN ENSKRUBBEN

Chimera *n* A fabulous monster of Greek mythogyny, with the head of a celebrity, the tongue of a serpent, the body of a cosmetic surgeon, and the tail of a Sicilian.

TED KOPPULATE

China *n* A dense farming community, gotten to by digging straight down from the intersection of I-75 and I-20, near the Atlanta bypass. It is said that if you lined up the population of China, five abreast, and marched them into a Ramada Inn, it wouldn't be any noisier.

MAO THALAWN

China Wall *n* A stonewall similar to the one in Deecee, America, but not as thickheaded.

Chinese puzzle *n* China.

Chiro *n* A combining form meaning "hand in another's pocket."

Chiropractic *n* A method of treating the imaginary diseases of the spine by manipulation of a patient, at the joints. The joints are called Life Clinics, where a chiropractor is pleased to improve his life by manipulating your bank account.

Choice *n* A previous freedom of America, available to a mountain man or a renegade Indian. Also, a mediocre grade of beef.

Cholesterol *n* A fatty crystalline substance, $C_{27}H_{45}I_{19}L_{69}I_{14}$. The most serious cause of flavor.

Christian Science A high technology by which a gunshot wound is correctly treated as any other psychosomasis or mental error. Devil Science, represented by the American Pharmaceutical Entrepreneurs Society, has put forward formal allegations of incredibility, and has suggested that if God had wanted Christians to be perfect He would have made them all M.D.'s.

Physician, heel, thyself!

MARY BAKER BROYLER

Christmas Eve *n* A night of prayer that the time of the closing of the department store shall pass quickly.

Christmas present *n* An afterthought-less blob of recycled refuse of half the value expected and a fifth of the cost allocated, mawkishly camouflaged to represent concern and support pretense. A gift of a wise man.

TINNY TIM

Chromatic aberration *n* A property of photographic lenses that causes people to appear in photographs as they really are, that is, off-colored. Compare
    Inebriatic aberration: wedding photographs
    Humdrumatic aberration: salon photographs
    Nikospastic aberration: professional photographs
    Acrobatic aberration: pornography

ANNA MORFIK

Church *n* A gambling hall offering mutual cards and lottery stubs on Wednesday nights. On Sundays an executive issues directives upon sociology.

D. BENCHURZ

Cigar *n* A serious delectation. According to Señor Feeno Panatella, Cuban women excel at the rolling of cigars. Prior to 1956 they also excelled at the rolling of cigar smokers.

A woman is only a drag,
but a good cigar is a toke.

SOCRATES

Cigarette *n* A paper tube formerly containing tobacco, and causing violent controversy among nonukers, abortionists, and the anti-gun lobbyists.

Cimmeria *n* A land described by Homer as a place of perpetual mist and darkness, extending from Venice, along the coast highway, through Santa Monica and Malibu, and ending at San Simian.

HEDDA BOPPER

Circe *n* An evil goddess who changed men into beasts and women into housewives.

Civil rights *n* The illegal entitlements of the Black, the Red, the Yellow, and the White to the plunder of the Suntanned. Universal sufferage.

Enough, enough of these damned slights!
I demand it all! the rights,
The flots and jets, the bytes
And harder wares that are now tuned
To proper spites, don't you see!
Old Rhetoric's noise will ply
The Straights, bring sights
Of quashed Responsibilities!

UMBRAGE MUGGERAGE

Clairvoyant *adj* Able to see into the next rent increase.

Clam *n* A medium of exchange:
    15 clams = 4 jumbo shrimp
    25 clams = 1 lobster tail (Professor Buyvalve
        informs us that up to 1974 you could still get
        a good piece of tail for only 10 clams.)

Clap *n* A reward for a performance (sometimes delayed).

Classics *n* Books bound in red leather, with gold pages, thoughtfully provided by Dickens, Melville, and Dostoyevsky to blend into the paneling of a family room. They are affixed, appropriately, above the people's magazine and other readers' indigestion racks, out of reach. *Syn* Wallpaper.

Clone *n* A manmade fraud resembling the original.

Clothes *n* A disguise affected by liars, cheats, and impostors. A moustache or beard is sometimes worn to delineate inhumanity.

                    VIDAL BABOON

Clouds *n* A docudrama by Aristophanes, concerning the failure of the sunglass and tanning-oil industries in Detroit.
    "I was depressed when I got here, but now I'm suicidal!"

           CHORUS OF CLOUDS, ACT II

Cockroach *n* A kitchen pest, smaller than a chef.

Coco Colo *n* An illegal narcotic derived from dung ash and coaltar, originally used to treat insomniac toads, but now trafficked among inebriates, adolescents, and condominiacs. Overdoses said to result in hyperawareness of warts and squash rackets, and glimpses of God. It is rendered harmless by the addition of rum.

Coffee *n* A putrescent ooze administered in restaurants as an antidote.

College education A product, inferior to fresh pasta or cubic zirconias, bought, at a discount, by consumers. *Syn* Hamburger; Ph.D.

Columbus, Chris *n* An explorer and naggravator.

> In fourteen hundred and ninety-two
> Columbus sailed the ocean green,
> Having naught else to do
> For Isabella, Queen.
> Three voyages made his name,
> And brought a fleeting fame;
> A fourth did thus reflect:
> "Born in Genoa,
>   Died in neglect."

MA JELLIN

Combat *n* The wanton destruction of property and irresponsible taking of human life, accounting for over 1.5 million slayings, sneak attacks, and suicides on the American highways alone, since 1950.

Occasional lapses allow young men to bask in the relative safety of war.

KAY OSZ

Combat zone   A horrid tract rife with booby traps, guns, sadism, terror, depression, paranoia, and fatigue; that is, a high school.

Comic book *n*   A best-seller, preferably by Bore Vidal, or a celebrity biography.

Comic opera *n*   A German one.

Comic relief *n*   A hiatus in serious business, as a session of Congress or a theory of economics.

Comic strip *n*   The disrobing of a human.

POLLY ESTHER

Commune *n*   A conscientious, calculating collective compound comprising a pavilion, called a Kibbutz, an elect staff, called Kibbitzers, and a product of their own labor, or a Kibbosh. Kibbitzers are also responsible for researching various markets to put the Kibbosh on, and they are usually successful. Communes are generally short-lived, especially in America, where they are known as Legislatures or Councils, and Kibbitzers there are usually concerned with putting the Kibbosh on every market of the economy.

JOHN KENNETH GALLBREATH

Communism *n*   A drabness of higher rank than Socialism. A system free of decadence and corruption, that is, wheat germ and sportsmen, but offering dignity to psychopaths.

Complacent *adj* Unable to initiate a treachery.

Completed pass *n* That where the defense is penetrated by the offense, often with a long ball.

OUY A. TITTLE

Complimentary *adj* Twice paid for.

Computer *n* An electrical machine that is able to produce the bungled miscalculations of a human one, at a faster rate.

All yield to the hasty computer!
How compelling! redoubtable! th' impetuous
tout 'er.
Incalculably inert,
Of certain no flirt,
But a chippy, no less, to a Boomer.
Obscure scrawl or logic symbolic,
Extend garbage-in to a promise triviolic.

BUMBER SCHUTZ

Concede *vt* To claim a moral victory.

Concert *n* Formerly a recital of Vivaldi, Liszt, or Rodrigo. Currently an assault of Volta and Hertz, Ohm and Watt.

Condense *vt* To reduce to 6500 words that which is tedious in 30.

PITTSBURGH AMORY

Condition *n* A state of preparedness for sale of an item of worth, of the hierarchy below:

    Clean: In pieces (3 missing), all pieces either dented, abraded, cracked, chipped, defaced, or deformed.

    Fair: In pieces (2 missing), all bent.

    Fair + : Wrong pieces (1 missing), remainder corroded.

    Good: Mechanism force-jammed; no parts available; surface rusted, blotched, scarred.

    Good + : Critical areas inoperable. Warped.

    Good ++ : Slight saltwater damage.

    Excellent: Surface blemishes. Dropped once only.

    Excellent +++ : Slight dent on master synchronizer plate and gear train retard mechanism. Serviceable in Ulan Bator only.

    Mint minus: Discontinued, recalled, twenty percent overpriced.

    Mint: Faded, scratched, needs overhaul. Ten percent above new retail price.

    As new: Abused, rubbed, dented.

    New: Used, compression-damaged; damaged in handling; damaged in shipping; bounced off receiving dock by Teamster. Illegally imported.

    Factory-fresh: Defective.

SAUL BUCK

Condominium *n* A shabby cell reserved for incorrigibles. *Abbr* condom.

Confession *n* A false document suppressed as bearing no relation to a retainer.

Connivial *adj* Of a happy affair where friends gather to drink generic Perriers, on separate checks, and backstab the competition. Compare **convivial**, of a false and devious sentiment leading to heinous consequences, as a dinner party.

Conscience *n* The kind of con that prohibits the correct attitude for success.

Consumer *n* One whose sole and eternal function is to consume, as a worm, an intestine, or a union man.

Contemporary *adj* Currently offensive.

Contempt *n* Suspicion, having grown up and left home.

Convenience *n* A modern expedient of people and automobiles.
> *Drivethru:* a golf course
> *Snorthru:* church service
> *Buythru:* college service
> *Trikthru:* dating service
> *Hypethru:* news service
> *Paythenosethru:* Legal service
> *Diarrhethru:* fast-food service
> ALDOUS HOAXLEY

Conversation *n* Verbal exchange. A dialogue between two speakers, as the following, between a citizen and an elitist:
> *Cit:* The stock market is—
> *Hon:* I buy only ivory, scrimshaw, snow

leopard pelts, panda rugs, and museum
pieces.
Cit: My vacation photos are—
MD: I've got a couple of Nikons.
Cit: Went fishing on my thirty-fifth birthday,
yesterday. It—
LLD: I've got a 36' Chris Craft.
Cit: Rent's going up again; they should—
CEO: Two of my condos are in Florida.
Cit: Bought one of those new lifetime batter-
ies, last—
Broker: I've got a black Eldorado with
leather interior.
Cit: What does the future hold for the arts?
Are they—
Celeb: I looked fantastic!

PHIL ABUZZTER

Cool (koō-ul, koō, kool) A word of 1–3 syllables
but no meaning.

Cordial *n* A prissy liquor for drinkers who prefer
a toothache to a hangover.

The feast was flocked, the guests were
crocked
And vice was all around;
It yelled and growled, and roared and howled
Where cordials did abound.
—*Rime of the Ancient Marnier*

Corpulent *adj* Stout.

On the occasion when a substantial fellow, of
some eight hundred fourteen pounds, and his wife,
of one hundred seventeen, were being tastelessly in-

terviewed by the tasteless host of a tasteless live morning TV talk show in Detroit, a cross-examination ensued from the prurient audience, the first predictable shot being fired by a tasteless suburban matron who righteously gushed, "Do you lead a normal sex life?"

"No, thank god!" was the answer.

HAMMOND WRY

Cosa Nostra *n* The most imposing force, in the world, that does not exist. The second most imposing force, in the world, that does not exist, is reason.

GUIDO RUTABAGA

Cosmetic surgeon *n* One who improves upon the mistakes of another god.

Cosmology *n* The vanity of reflection. Compare the higher **cosmetology,** the language of the stars.

Cost overrun *n* An oversight in fiscal tailoring, attributed to a miscalculation in the size of the suit and the number of pockets to be lined.

VENARABLISS

Cough *n* A staccato impervious, in music halls, to interruptions of noise from the stage.

Counter attack The result of a counter meal.

Coup *n* (Fr, brilliant stroke) In popular usage it refers to the taking over of a government.

 Coup d'état: Govt. takeover by the military
 Coup de'sgrace: Govt. takeover by the press

Coup de theatre: Govt. takeover by politicians
Coup de tarde: Govt. takeover by the post office
Coup de mirrour: Govt. takeover by women
Coup de bulleur: Govt. takeover by actors

FIDEL KENNEDY

Covert *adj* The activities of the American intelligence community, to the relief of other dictatorships who had thought them to be secret.

Crab *n* A shellfish animal found at exclusive and epicurean clubs.

According to the highly credentialed Chef Robbere, the cost of the single delicacy is quite high, though a case of crabs is still obtainable for about twenty-five dollars.

Cracker barrel An empty container surrounded, commonly, by empty heads.

Beat an empty barrel,
Pound an empty head.

VACHEL HERESAY

Crepe *n* A trendy pancake. A nontrendy pancake is a panflap, a jackcake, a hotstack, a griddlecake, or a tirepatch (silver-dollar pancake).

UNCLE JEMIMA

Crevice *n* A crack or fissure encountered while mountain climbing. Compare crevass, a mountain climber.

Criminal lawyer *n* A particular kind of criminal.

Crisis *n* A common catchword in the language of the primitive Jurinalese, of Nettwurx. It refers to the trafficking of sensational gossip, rather than customary.

ABIE SEA

Crocodilian *adj* Of a family of primitive reptiles that includes the crocodile, the alligator, the gavel, and the layman.

Cro-Magnon *adj* Relating to a species of pre-Beaujolais Frenchmen.

Cross *n* Singly, a symbol of hope. Doubled, it is even more hopeful (and popular).

RINGO REAGAN

Crown *n* A trinket that separates the king from the rest of the court fools. *Syn* limo.

Cruise *n* A passage of voyeurgers.

Cryptogram *n* A communication in indecipherable gibberish, as the works of Faulkner, or the tax laws.
I seed de printin'
And I seed de scribin',
But I ain't seed nothin' that looks like
writin'.

AUNTIE BELAM

Cubicle *n* An office designed in the shape of an executive.

Cubism *n* An art form characterized by the use of geometrical patterns rather than by a realistic portrayal of nature, as in Sure-realism and Sure-dadaism.

> I have no powders, only solutions;
> Hello, Dali!

> MAN TARAY

Cubit An ancient insult done by motioning with the length of the arm, from the middle finger to the elbow.

> Cube it!

> PABLO PISTACHIO

Culture *n* In America, something found in a test tube at MIT. Elsewhere, a manner of talking.

> PEEWEE SANTAYANA

Cuneiform *adj* Pertaining to an ancient writing whose characters were formed with the use of golf tees, obtained from the links that extended from Assyria to Persia and Pebble Beach to Babylonia.

Some common symbols:

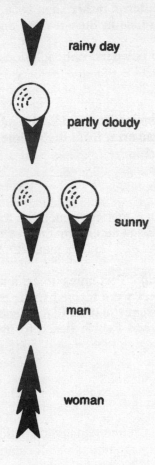

rainy day

partly cloudy

sunny

man

woman

Cynic *n* A superman, with x-rayted vision. Invulnerable.

LOIS LAIN

d

Dakin's solution *n* A mildly alkaline solution of sodium hypochlorite, used to heal a wound. Compare **Deacon's solution,** a wildly asinine solution of a podium hypocritite, used to wound a heel.

Damnides *n* (Gr, starlets) According to legend, the fifty daughters of San Fernando and Gyptus, who at their father's command divorced their producer-husbands and were therefore condemned in Hollywood to pour drinks forever at a Howard Johnson Motor Lodge.

Dangerous chemical An average of 92–190 pounds of vested protoplasm, worth an inflationary amount of about $11.43, soaking wet.

Data *n*
Dā′tə	Common misinformation
Dat′ə	Ambitious misinformation
Dä′tə	Elite misinformation

Dawn *n* The time at which night noises cease and day noises begin. *Syn* Debbie, Skip, Nikki.

Day care *n* The abuse of a foundling; while at night a sitter sees to kidnappers.

Dead center The area lying above the superior maxillary and anterior to the parietal.

Dead-letter office *n* A library.

Deadline *n* A line of newsprint noting an author.

Dead reckoning *n* The method of navigation used by an automobile driver.

Deaf *adj* Deprived of discord.

Death *n* A disorder of the brain, occurring at puberty, as the intestines and genitals proceed as the seat of reason for the remainder of life, or adulltery.

Deb *n* The diminutive of Debbie, a girl's name. The other girl's name is Sue.

Debtor's prison *n* An awful, tacky place, full of unspeakable horrors, brutality, and deceit: noisy, with no privacy, and containing four bedrooms, two and a half baths, a family room, six teevees, a breakfast nook, and a Jacuzzi.

Deceptive packaging Skin *(Epidermis inhumanis).*

CHRISTIAN LATH, M.D.
RHINOPLASTERER TO THE STARS

Decidua *n* A membrane found in the human uterus during pregnancy and cast off at birth, usually weighing between five and eight pounds.

Defenestration *n* Rapid descent unencumbered by an elevator.

Dehorn *vt* To remove the horn or horns from. This process is regularly proposed and occasionally carried out by certain vociferous dehorners, the most prominent being the devout Damsels of God's Service (D.O.G.S.), who are mighty afeared of getting stuck, though a kindly providence has furnished them with a natural immunity.

ANN APPLUS

Delinquent *adj* Ahead of the game.

Delirium tremens *n* An unpopular form of hallucination, decried by the younger set.

Demigod *n* The offspring of a human being and a celebrity.

Demoralize *vt* To discourage or corrupt. To affix with a job. To make a friend.

De mortuis nil nisi bonum *n* (L) Of the dead say nothing good.

Denouement *n* The unraveling of a carelessly woven fabric, usually weblike.

Deodorant *n* A delousing agent used to protect innocent microbes from their treacherous hosts.

Depression *n* A low place in the interstate, such as Detroit, Chicago, or Fort Laudertail.

Deregulate *vt* To promote the spirit of free competition by dividing a large monopoly into several smaller ones, in order to benefit the public by raising prices and eliminating services.

PA BELL

Derelict *n* One who retired before the mandatory age, and thus assumed a reduction in benefits.

Designer *n* One who, with needle and thread, makes designs on your wallet.

OSCAR RAESTHARENTA

Detox *n* A fashionable haunt of former notables. It lies in Beverly's Hills, between press agents.

OLIVIA NEWTON FIG

Deviate *n* There are two types of deviate: the homosexual and the heterosexual, the former addicted to perversions against another fool, and the latter to the rape of an opposite.

Devil's playground *n* An area at the rear of a high school, next to the parking lot. See also **High School.**

Diabolical *adj* Diabolic; mischievous; pertaining to other than standard fiendishness.

X. S.

Diana *n* The goddess of hunting and virginity, unknown in North America.

Dicotylyzitofylerazonous *adj* Having two cotylyzitofylerazons.

Diet *n* A regimen undertaken for the improvement or stability of health. The following are selections from a reasonable and effective seven-day diet, containing all the recommended daily doses of essential nutrients for the maintenance of equilibrium while toting a briefcase or stethoscope: condensed from *Reader's Dietjest* by the noted Hellenic nutritionist, Prof. Ethel Enemadiamines:

Monday breakfast (accompanied by Vivaldi's
   Concerto in D for Guitar)
   glass of diet juice:
      1.5 oz diet gin
   7 oz orange juice (freshly squeezed)
   1 large wedge diet apple pie
   1 large wedge diet sharp cheddar cheese
   2 cups diet coffee (non-caffein-free, black)
   3 diet cigarettes
      allowable 10:30 A.M. snack: 1 Godiver
      chocolate: $35.00
Monday lunch (accompanied by assorted Bach
   partitas)
   glass of diet juice:
      2 oz diet vodka

    1 oz lime juice (freshly squeezed)
    4 oz diet tonic water
2 diet cigarettes
2 large diet Alaskan sockeye salmon patties (diet cucumber garnish)
5 oz diet fresh mashed potatoes
8 oz diet creamed pea sauce
3 slices diet crusty French bread (4–6 oz diet unsalted butter)
1 very large wedge diet chocolate soufflé
12 oz diet premium current Soave
2 diet cigarettes
    allowable 3:45 P.M. snack: 1 Bill Blast bonbon: $29.50

Monday dinner (accompanied by Verdi's *Nabucco)*

assorted fresh diet fruits and diet cheeses
bottle of Wachenheimer Gerumpel spätlese (any good diet year)
1 diet José Melendi Epicure

Wednesday breakfast (accompanied by Bach's Brandenburg Concerto No. 1)

glass of diet juice:
    1.5 oz diet rum
    5 oz pineapple juice (freshly squeezed)
sliced fresh diet peaches and ripe diet bananas
1 peanut butter granola bar
4 cups diet coffee (non-caffein-free, black)
5 diet cigarettes
    allowable 10:30 A.M. snack: 1 oz pâté: $3.75 (with scent of truffle: $126.75)

Wednesday lunch (accompanied by *Patsy Cline's Greatest Hits)*

glass of diet juice:
  2 oz diet tequila
  .05 oz diet triple sec
  1 oz lemon-lime juice (freshly squeezed)
  4 oz diet cracked ice
  salt to taste (use unsalted diet salt)
2 diet cigarettes (unfiltered)
2 diet chile rellenos
3 diet enchiladas
ladle of diet refried beans
1 portion (9 oz) rice
36 oz diet draft beer
1 Te-Amo cheroot (diet ring size 5)
  allowable 4 P.M. snack: 1 oz Smithfield
  ham: $63.00
Wednesday dinner (accompanied by Andreas
Vollenweider's *Caverna Magica)*
poached cherries and cantaloupe baskets
bottle of diet Cockburn's Alto Douro port
1 Partagas diet No. 8
Friday breakfast (accompanied by Paganini's
24th Caprice)
glass of diet juice:
  2.5 oz diet Yukon jack
  3 oz clam juice (freshly squeezed)
  2.5 oz diet Yukon jack
6 oz creamed diet chipped beef on a toasted
  shingle
2.5 oz Yukon jack
6 cups diet coffee (non-caffein-free, black)
2 parodis
  allowable 10:30 A.M. snack: 3 silver-dollar

pancakes: 79¢ (with pure maple syrup:
$11.50)

Friday lunch   (accompanied by Liszt's 6th
Hungarian Rhapsody)
glass of diet juice:
  1 oz diet shot
  12 oz diet beer
2 diet cigarettes
20 oz diet lobster thermidor
fresh diet raspberry bombe
16 oz diet Gewürztraminer d'Alsace (current
  diet year)
1 diet Montecristo cetro (legally imported by
  an ACLU lawyer)
  allowable 4:00 P.M. snack: 2 pistachios:
  $7.00

Friday dinner   (accompanied by Bizet's *Carmen*
—Maria Callas)
2 bottles diet Hungarian Tokay (7 puttonos, 2
  glasses)
.13 Karl Upmann diet lonsdale (stolen from
  Canadian embassy by ghetto congressman)

Sunday breakfast   (accompanied by *Harry Ja-
nos,* Beethoven's *32 Variations, Coppélia, Syl-
via, Les Sylphides,* and *Rigoletto)*
glass of diet juice:
  1 oz papaya juice (freshly squeezed)
  1 oz mamaya juice (freshly squeezed)
  12 oz diet light rum
  12 oz diet dark rum
  12 oz diet medium rum
  1 egg substitute (small)
40 Dromedary cigarettes

Have a healthy day!
Sincerely,

ETHEL ENEMADIAMINES PH.D., WITH CHEF
ROBBERE

Dignity *n*   The Tree of Life, cut down by Civilization and bulldozed to the Mill of Society, where it is whittled to the Toothpick of Despair.

Dik-Dik *n*   A small African Richard-Richard.

Dilute *vt*   To weaken by admixture; e.g., to spoil bourbon with water.

Dime *n*   A former U.S. silver coin, worth six cents, or a tenth of two dollars.

DimeNasty *n*   A popular TV novel and continuing saga of the Carryingdungs of Denver. As the new season unfolds we find that Alezis mysteriously develops bunions on her eyelids and is forced to retire to a theme nunnery in Watervliet, where she opens a designer leather boutique for sizes 6–9 exclusively (closed Mondays). At a celebrity fundraiser for Orientals unable to grow sideburns, she meets and falls in love with a bisexual Sherpa from Backbay who eventually becomes the Tofutti king of the Eastern Seaboard and throws her over for the Guinness World Record holder in the Sitting-in-a-Buick-and-Necking-in-August-with-the-Windows-Rolled-Up-and the Heater-on-Having-Not-Bathed-in-a-Month category—300 lb and over Division. Vengefully, Alezis, through the influence of Sen.

Hackle, whom she met limping out of the out-patient clinic of the Georgetown Center for Untreatable Venereal Diseases, wearing a Groucho Marx mask and a hangover, on Father and Daughter Night, has the Tofutti king's "green card" pulled; whereupon he is deported to Redondo Beach to languish as an image consultant for Thomas Noguchi (who by this time has a pretty decent set of sideburns).

Bleke, who learns that his real father was Rondo Hatton, "the Creeper," is spotted by his moustachioed ex–daughter-in-law, Sammi-Jimmi, coming out of an exhibition parlor in Oak Park, carrying Alezis's new spring catalog, a fuzzy block-and-tackle, a black pump size 14EEE, a 25¢ discount coupon for a gallon of E-Z-DUZ-IT mineral oil, and an autographed photo of Renee Richards. He ducks into his Marye-Kaye Cadillac and roars off to an invitational lecture and motivation seminar during Middle-American Virtue Week at the Thomas Road Church, where he is shocked to discover that the pink Caddie he's been driving is really a $695 kit car, with phony whitewalls and a Hamilton-Beach engine. Meanwhile, in Denver, Bleke's corporation is subjected to an unfriendly takeover by the shadowy hermaphrodite eyebrow-waxer whom Bleke suspects is the second offspring of his hushed marriage to Countess Ouwtt, charismatic chairwoman of the Department of Rubber Studies at the University of Stockholm.

Krysdull, fresh from a gig as a volunteer sphygmomanometer monitor and blue-follicle coordinator at a low-sodium convention in Sun City, finds fulfillment at a limbo tournament in Vail as she is swept off her feet by a gay oyster-shucker from the Hamptons, in for the cheesecake season, who turns out to be Bleke's long-lost son from an affair with Creole Cleo, the "toast of the Hojo coast." Determined to make a go of this new relationship, after she gives birth to Bleke's chief accountant's child, Krysdull becomes the social director at Vacaville to be close to Rambeau Serealsnuffr, a professor of genealogy who went mad while in the Carryingdung's employ, and to whom she made the promise that she would devote the rest of her life to jazzercise.

Ed. note: Sammi-Jimmi bolted to join the cast of *The Young and the Arrested.*

LOU WOW

Dingbat *n* A doohickey, formerly a thingamabarb; as distinguished from **ol-bat,** which is a gimcrack or a gewgaw; and **brickbat,** a flibbergibbet. Dingbats are sometimes mistaken for ol-bats and flapdoodles, although ol-bats exhibit a characteristic blue-widgetry, and dingbats are usually more thingy or dingalingous.

Dinner Theater *n* A situation leaving a bad taste in one's mouth about acting.

LEE STRASSENBAHNBURG

Diogenes *n* A Greek who lived in a cold tub while searching, with a lantern, for an honest plumber.

Directory *n* A phone aid, known, commonly, as the Hello Pages. The following is a list of important phone numbers for the convenience of those not possessed of a Hello Pages:

Information: 1-800-555-CROK
Fire: 1-800-555-ARSN
Ambulance: 1-800-555-RIPP
Sheriff: 1-800-555-TAKE
Poison Control: 1-800-222-LATE
Coast Guard Rescue: 1-800-555-GLUG
Suicide Prevention: 1-800-555-JUMP
Secret Service: 1-800-292-
Legal Aid: 1-800-555-VEST
Dial-a-Prayer: Area code 213-812-JOKE
Dial-a-Date: 1-800-555-DOGG
Acme Telemarketing Svc.: 1-800-555-PEST
Gen. Emergency: 1-800-555-214--888-777-999-
626-534-755-911-MORG

Disadvantaged *adj* Imperfectly greedy.

Documentary *n* A film made without actors, and thus credible, while a narrator lies about issues.
WALTER CRANKTIGHT

Dodo *n* A large flightless bird related to the auk of Nova Scotia and the gawk of Shaker Heights, and thought to be extinct; however, occasional sightings have been reported as far south as Los Angeles, Salt Lake City, and Newark, in the vicinity of voting booths.

Dog-eat-dog *n* An expression of middle-class dogs.

Dogfood *n* An entrée provided by the elite for bitches and curs, that is, retirees.

MAXIM FWAGRA

Dolce far niente (Ital) It takes nine bishops to equal one devil.

Dolce vita, la (Ital) The dolt taketh the vitamin.

VATICAN INSCRIPTIONS

Dolphin *n* An animal *(homo seaworldus)* with a brain nearly the size of that of a human *(Homo preposterens)*, but possessing reason.

Dominus vobiscum (L) The Lord be with me while I bet the lottery.

Doomsday Book *n* The registry of holy offenders, formerly maintained in heaven, but which became so ponderous, with the advent of evangelism, Wall Street, and celebrity biographies, that it had to be lowered to a more constant environment, and now rests in the Library of Congress.

Doomsday Clock *n* A faulty timepiece stuck at two minutes to midnight, which is 5:00 P.M. in the District of Columbia.

Doomsday Machine An engine of hell, said to be similar to a VCR or a cordless telephone. Senator Taeque insists that it is not unlike a platoon of male ballet dancers, while Ambassador Anatoly Jzczerkov says that it is probably closer to a beauty pageant or a Loco Cola.

Dos-à-dos *n* A movement in square dancing where two contestants approach each other, exchange doses, and return to their original positions.
JOHNNY CREDITCARD

Douse *vt* To extinguish a fire. Compare **souse,** to start one.

> Wherefore McGee, a pyrotechnician,
> Rose to instruct in tavernous fission,
> As with four double-shots he soused it,
> And with a pail of beer he doused it.
>
> JOHN BARELYCORN

Dr. *n* In America, an Indian or Pakistani who cannot understand poor English, but is conversant with profit. In India or Pakistan, an American specialist in bleeding hearts. In powder rooms, a "catch."

Dr. J. *n* A superstar. An inimitable performer, having courted the favor of numerous galleries of discriminating fans, with another Great Dictionary.
J. BOSWELL

Driver's license *n* A warrant of homicide issued at puberty, and irrevocable.

Drug-dependent *n* A son or daughter.

Drug-free *adj* Out of money.

Drunk *n* A past partitipple. Listed below are some fundamental formulae.

Cuba Libre: Rum, cloak-a-cola, salt-petre, charcoal, sulfur, and a wedge of napalm.

Black Russian: Kalashnikov vodka and a Kabullion cube.

White Russian: Polish vodka on the rocks, with a twist of Lenin.

Tequila Sunrise: Tequila, orange juice, scrambled eggs, tortillas, and coffee; consumed at dawn, before being shot.

B-52: 1 shot of Kentucky bourbon per crew member, served over cracked ice-otopes. Garnished with a mushroom. (Also called B-1, conservatively.)

Buck: A drink passed from sot to sot, then on to the next party.

JIM FIZZ
HARVEY BALLWHANGER

Drunk driver *n* One with the best view of the crash.

Ducking Stool *n* A cruel and human punishment, no longer fashionable, where a gossip is forced to feel a duck then eat a crow.

Dumb show *n* A play done without speech, as the ones in New York City, but, according to high sources, not without mumbling.

NOEL COWHERD

Dumpster *n* Poverty's bassinet.

e

Ear piercing   A vulgar ritual of savages and egolitarians residing on either side of the Isthmus of Blare, near the Tropic of Commotion. Components used are diamond needles, by the backward, while more malicious enthusiasts employ lasers to achieve the desired effect of a ringing in a victim's ears.

MONTE VIDEO

Earring *n*   An article of human adornment once thought to be worn by only one of the sexes, but now known to be used by all four.

Easy listener *n*   An aficionado whose favorite composer is Musak or Dulby or Volume.

HORACE TUKATTEAU

Ecology *n*   The biological science of living things and their irrelevance to the interstate highway.

TOM TIT

Economical *adj*   A modern term describing the common man's inaccessibility to the premium of Worth.

Edinburgh *n*   (*pron* Edinburro) A capital city near the Firth of Forth and Fifth of Scotch. Not to be confused with the small suburb of **Ednburg** *(pron* Edinburrito).

Ejaculate *vt* To utter abruptly, by mistake; to discharge a fluid abruptly, by mistake.

Element *n* There are four elements left: earth, air, bourbon, and water.
"Those who drink are of the pure element."
BLASSFEMES

Eligible Bachelorette *n* One who lies in wait for Mr. Right, M.D.

Elixir *n* A panacea. A substance dispensed to hopheads by medieval sorcerers as a remedy for all ailments. Modern sorcerers also prescribe Valium.

Elocution *n* The putting to death of a good word gone bad. The elocutioner sometimes wears a mask.
SIR LAURENCE OLIVIOIL

Elope *n* A congenitally blind burrowing animal, sometimes nocturnal in its habits. Distinguished from an antelope, a wise being of much better vision, and fleeter of foot.

Emission(s) *n* There are four kinds of emission(s): international, federal, Californian, and nocturnal, the latter two producing the foulest contaminants known to nature.

Employee *n* One usable. According to Ms. Faztrak, of Swelling and Smelling, Inc., all future employees will be 28-year-old college-educated black Catholic divorced childless female Democrats with letterpressed résumés composed of code words and action verbs.

KARL BARX

Encephalitis lethargica *n* Sleeping sickness. Compare **Encephalitis consumerica,** waking sickness; **Encephalitis jurisprudica,** dozing sickness.

Entertain *vt* To elevate from boredom to disgust.

Epaulet *n* Something resting on the shoulders of a military officer; usually the most important thing.

Epigram *n* According to the magnificent and definitive *Oxford Universall Dictionary* (1782) "a small cutlet, dressed in a sauce." With the singular assistance of this liberated lexicon's consulting gastrognome and culinier, Chef Robbere, we provide the following entrées, being familiar cuts dressed in an improved sauce:

Education is what is left over after you have fired all the teachers.

PLATOSTOTLE

One man, one vote. One woman, two democratic votes, or three.

THOMAS PAIN

We shall overcharge, we shall overcharge, we shall overcharge every day and keep the sucker's pay.

MARTIN LUTHER NIXON

You can always sell a Harvard man, but you can't get much.

ANON

You can lead a Harvard man to water, but you can't make him sink.

TEDDY KENNY

It is a newspaper's duty to slant the news and praise hell.

BULLITZER PULLITZER

Money is the root of all pleasure.

ARMAND CHISELL

Out of sight, out of optometrists.

BLINKY CHARTZ

Man may work from sun to sun,
but woman's work is never.

GLORIA STONEM

A fool and his money are soon taxes.

IRA ASSE

The customer is always trite.

HUGH MUNGOS

Love conquers all: and doesn't take prisoners.

M. FAZEEMA

Hell hath no fury like a woman's corn.

ORVILLE POPPERBOCKER

There's a taxpayer born every minute.

P. T. DARNEM

Stand up and be dis-counted.

MOAMMAR K. DAFFY

Vanity, thy name is profits.

D. ZYNER

You never know!

SPINWHEELZA

Thirty days hath September: leaving 335 more in which to be in a daze.

MAY ZWELLE

Smile and the world smiles with you: frown and you finally get some peace and privacy.

PERRY O. DONTIX

Smile and the world smiles with you; frown
and some smiler will eventually pester you.

RAQUEL TEETH

Smile and the world smiles with you: frown
and you will attract an Amway Rep.

FRAN CHEIZ

My compliments to the can opener.

CHEF ROBBERE

The pen is mightier than the slam.

SAM QUENTIN

If a literary man puts together two words about
music, one of them will be first.

ERRIN' COBLAND

Truculence, thy name is Physician!

CAD SCAN

Never give a sucker an even break: make it a
compound fracture, and go for the insurance!

O. D. BODKIN, M.D.

There's no arrest for the wicked.

MOE TAVEAT

All things come to him that waits, then takes
by force.

SCHMIT & WESSON

Always a bridesmaid, never a divorcee.

DIRE ABBY

Turnabout is foreplay.

BUBBLES MACARTHUR

What tools these mortars be!

QUEDAFFY ARABFAT

The grass always looks greener on a private
golf course.

JACK CLUBHAUS

A day in Detroit is a day without sunshine.

ANITA NAVEL

There's no such thing as a free salad bar.

COLONEL SLANDERS

A woman should be a gossip in the family room; a defroster in the kitchen; and a whore in the shower.

JACQUES COOZIE

Never argue with a person who doesn't have a neck.

VINCE BOMBARDI

Tomorrow is some other day.

YOGI YEVTUSHENKO

All the world loves a franchise.

MARY K. PATHETIC

Service is our middle name (but our first name is Bad).

ARCHIE PELLAGO

Time flies when you're having phone.

TELEMARKETER'S CREED

A bachelor is a man who never made the same mistake once.

FRA LIPPO LIPPMAN

Man shall not live by bread alone. Give him beans and taxes.

RUSEAFELT

Hesoever that believeth in me shall cut the mustard.

SID HARTHA

Epitaph *n* An epigram with a nose for worms.
Here lies Lester Moore,
Four slugs from a forty-four,
No Les, no more.

BOOT HILL

Ashes to ashes, dust to dust,
If smoking won't kill me,
In God I'll trust—
So when I die place upon my breast,
A '66 La Tour,
And chisel, "Optopest."

BOOT VALLEY

E pluribus unum *n* Out of many the withholding.

U.S. MOTTO

Equality *n* A cesspool of virtue. *Syn* America. *Ant* Democracy.

Equal opportunity *n* The prospect of pillage for the meek.

Equal rights *n* The weightiest concern of an American, after salad bars, collector's items, lotteries, and rolling papers.

Equestrienne *n* A woman who performs with a horse, which is quite a sight.

Equinox *n* A time of year when day and night are equally tedious and when astronomers and philosophers are able to stand an egg on end. The bacon strips are said to be slightly more difficult.

E. KLIPTIK

Erebus *n* (Gr. myth) The bus that transports the dead under the earth and through Hades, before entering Atlantic City. N.Y. Transit Auth. No. 69.

Erudite *adj* (Ef-rē-yoo-dīt)   A three-syllable word restricted to the use of a boob.

Est modus in rebus   (L) Jury tampering is a virtue.

WHORACE

Estriol *n*   A female sex hormone, $C_{18}H_{24}E_{11}A_{39}T_{13}$.

Ethics *n*   A system of conduct recommended by politicians, lawyers, and philosophers to their opponents.

D.V.S.

European plan *n*   An international system by which hotel guests are charged for room noise but pay for typhoid separately. Popular in Mazatlán.

Eurydice *n*   (Gr leg) A nymph. The wife of Orpheus. After she was killed, Orpheus gained permission to bring her back from Hades, via Anaheim, but she was forced to return because Orpheus broke his agreement with Pluto by hiring a private detective to see if she was followed by Mickey or Goofy.

Euthanasia *n*   A method of homicide employed where surgery fails.

Evil *n*   The evening clothes of Foolishness.

Evil I *n*   The first-person singular evil.

Evolution *n* The progression and advancement of species, such as worms to toads, toads to shrews, shrews to apes, apes to men, and men to jackasses.

CHARLES DARLOSE

Excess *n* Sufficiency. "Nothing too excessive."

ZENO

Existence *n* The excretion of infinities.

Ex nihilo nihil fit (L) It is fitting that from nothing man returns.

ST. IGNATIUS OF PAYOLA

Exorcism *n* The drawing off of excess evil from the soulless and possessed, that is, non-Christians. It is performed by raising the voice and scaring the devil. According to the council of Esoffagis, in 1893 the Jesuits of Detroit cast out 4,392 devils, who were then scourged and forced to incorporate the suburbs of Grosse Pointe; however, some of the devils escaped to the Dearborn asylums. Brother Peonite insists that viable demons to this day inhabit the two-digit residences of Lakeshore Drive.

Exotic food Something rarely, if ever, consumed, such as a steak cooked the way you ordered it.

CHEF ROBBERE

Extol *vt* To praise, in hope of payment. Compare **execrate**, to praise having received payment.

Extravaganza *n* A superfluous vaganza.

Exuberance *n* A defect of character in those prone to exhibitions of salesmanship, fits of social-awareness, or other excesses, dissipations, theme parties, pre-theater suppers, career opportunities, and fund-raisers. According to Prof. Rap Skalyan of Wane State, the foible is correctible by banning brunch hostesses and motivation seminars for a period of seven years.

ENGELHUMP BURBERDINCK

Exurbanite *n* (Coined 1955 in D.C. by A. C. Specterski) An unemployable drifter of the upper lower class who resides in a sleazy condo beyond those of the suburbs, but who commutes to New York or L.A. as a media consultant.

Eyes *n* The windows of the sold.

Eye witness *n* One whose faulty vision is brought, by subpoena, to the focus of an adversary.

CLARENCE NARROW

f

Fabrication *n* A lie with postdoctoral credentials.

Face *n* The part of the human anatomy most supportive of egg.

Facilis descensus Averno (L) The decent easily go to hell.

VIRGIL

> A true goddess, her walk revealed it,
> But, alas, her mouth concealed it.
> Speak to me, O Queen! Is hell
> The fate of decent Trojans? Swell!
> Then there's the rub, the glad tears,
> As I leave this mortal vale,
> The payments on the Chevy in arrears.
> PUBLIUS GLUTEUS PROFUNDUS

Fairy tale *n* Romance, job satisfaction, stress management, privacy, money in the bank, and other grims.

Fakir *n* A holyman whose duty it is to beg; opposed to **evangelist,** whose holiness is conjectural. Variously pronounced.

Falstaff *n* A medieval magician who could turn wine into urine.

Familiarity *n* A breed of contempt indulged in by the Medias.

Fanatic *n* A misguided infidel who murders in the name of Religion rather than in the holy cause of Off-Shore Oil Leases.

WILLIAM RANDOLPH HEIST

Fantastic *adj* Egregious. *Syn* huh, wow, yanoe.
>The sweet twitter of verbiage mundastic,
>Reiterate slosh of the popular fan; spastic
>Performances of nonstop nightly mumblastics,
>And what was coming from shooters bullshastic,
>Of friends and fit-ins hypercrastic;
>Smoke from the inebriate parade of ludicrastics,
>Ya-know the righteous dullastics,
>Was simply too, too, too fantastic!

TOOTS SHEETZ

Fast food *n* The kind that makes its way from mouth to bowl in less than nine minutes.

5.2 BILLION SERVED

Faun *n* (*Faunus*, Pan) A minor deity presiding over Bombast, Incoherence, and Halls of Fame, and possessing the head of an ape, the body of a producer, the horns and tail of a democrat, and reared by an ass. A faun is commonly seen brandishing a microphone or other engine of noise and disruption, and is sometimes taken for a Satr, or Star.

Faux pas (Fr) A social blunder, as in the attending of a social function or the encouragement of small talk. Compare the nefarious **gran pas,** a house party.

AMY BLANDERBUILT

FDA *n* Felonious Druggists of America.

Feminism *n* The theory that feminists should have political, social, and economic rights equal to those of other men.

Film *n* The title taken by trash whose budget is less than a million dollars. Trash with a budget of more than a million dollars is called **cinema.**

SAL U. LLOYD

Finishing school *n* An institution for girls that does its job.

Fishing *n* An inactivity charitably described by the distinguished Samuel Johnson as "a worm angling for a fool," or thereabouts. Modern fools have access to high-tech equipment for fishing, and are known to, in the case of some intractable flounders, rebut the hook and line with a pistol: though they are then cursed publicly as "hunters," rather than "philosophers," as is wont. Izaak Walton's *The Compleate Lawyere, or The Contemptible Man's Recreation,* is concerned with angling in the seventeenth century.

WILLE DONNE

Fixed *adj* Appropriately misadjusted. Spayed or neutered. Compare **fixed income,** an income from which the ovaries or testicles have been removed in preparation for a different kind of screwing.

ANNE EUITEA

Flamboyant *adj* Said of a crook when the shirt is silk and the tongue silver.

Flathead Indians A highly intelligent North American council, of the Bitterroot Range, whose language is of the Salishan. The city of Seattle is named for their great chief, Garfield Kootenay. Compare **Flatheaded aborigines,** an irresponsible tribe, of the Rootless Range, near Arlington, whose language is Salacious. The city of Pentagon is named for their great chief, General Imbroglio.

Flock *n* A herd having said its prayers.

Floorwalker *n* An executive who directs business in a department store. Compare **streetwalker,** an entrepreneur with a much greater sphere of influence.

Florence Nightingale (1820–1910) Inventor of cold hands.

Flying Dutchman A cruiser said to operate on a skeleton crew.

HOPE GOODCAPE

Fog *n* A layer of air that hovers about 5′9″ off the ground. According to Prof. Nimbus, it is composed of elements of phenepherins, caffeins, salicylates, phenols, cannabis, cocas, assetaminophens, bayrum and transistors. *Syn* "cloud nine."

Folsom man *n* A member of a race *(Homo penitensis)* believed to have existed in California during the Electro-Gasiferous Age.

Fool *n* A survivor. A misconception, of a tantalizing blend of trendy boorishness, numskulduggery, and pretense, with a record short jestation period.

U. FAMIZZEM

"For a good time call Trixie, Kristie, Morgan, or Liz at 555-1800 (competitive prices)." Propositional phrase.

Forte *n* A peculiar competency.
> Hark! The celibritous hordes bray
> The insidious belch of " 'Tis my forte!"
> And condescend that bilious snort,
> But leave unscathed our brave, proper forte.

HENRY THOROUGH

"For your convenience" For my profit.

Foster mother A woman who acts as a mother to a child not her husband's own. *Syn* wife.

Foumart *n* The European polecat. Compare **kaymart,** the American polecat.

Foundling *n* A child abandoned and left to the whims of parents.

Four-letter word *n* Any of several words dealing with pornography or excrement and regarded as being objectionable and unprintable, as: *press, lib, media, commie, video, candidate, superstar, tax.*

MARLON BRANFLAKE

Free *adj* Exorbitantly costly. Defective. Overpriced.

Freedom *n* The opportunity to be swindled by a democrat; as distinguished from **totalitarianism,** which is indiscriminate.

Freeway *n* A tributary of gore feeding the reservoirs of hell.

French and Indian War *n* A scuffle that occurred between the English and the French, in America. It lasted from 1754 to 1764, and thus became known as the Seven Years War.

Freudian slip A regalia lurking beneath the Freudian robe, and occasionally showing itself. It is not known for sure whether Freud wore a brassiere.

JUNG and WRESTLESS

Frigidity *n* Female impotence, currently unpopular and unexploitable.

Frontier *n* A place uncorrupted, that is, uninhabited, by a petroleum geologist.

Full bore *n* A celebrity, after dessert.

Fumble *n* In a football game, a rehearsed move that allows the other team to catch up to the point spread. Compare **mumble**, a player's news conference after a football game.

THE FOUR WHORSEMEN

Fun *n* The mirth of viciousness.

Furies *n* (Gr myth) Seven terrible female spirits with snaky hair and incoherent speech (Megaera, Alecto, Tisiphony, Shaer, Kristy, Liz, and Jane) who punished media groupies and sought awful vengeance in chain bookstores.

EUMENIDES, after EURIPIDES

Futility *n* A sinew given regular exercise by the faithful.

g

Galatea *n* (Gr leg) A full-size ivory statue come to life when Pygmalion, under the influence of an aphrodisiac, proposed equal rights to it, thereby reducing its value from 3000 silver drachmae to 59 cents.

GEO. BERNARD PSHAW

Game show *n* A show of consumers swooning at Mixmasters, sheet metal, and automated dish-scrubbers; and where human dignity is fair game.

BOB BARFER

Gang *n* An urban committee presiding over social mobility and redistribution of extortion. Members are forced to live among rats and garbage, that is, councilmen and mayors, and subsist on low-income homicides.

Garbage man The informal phylogenetic reference to a North American.

Garnish *n* A distraction incredible for an entrée inedible.

DUNCANS HIND

Gene *n* The illegitimate legacy of an impostor.

Germany *n* A country divided by mutual Soviet consent.

Get *n* The second-highest deity in the pantheon of the aborigines of Sillaburbia *(Homo bingonensis)*, the supreme godhead being Bet, a Holy Roller residing in a tawdry palace near Hoover's damn, whose handmaids are Grab and Gawk, and to whom are attended the rites of the Humiliation of the Table and the Sacrament of the Slots.

G. GULCH

Ghoti *n* George's Hoary Old Titillating Idiom.

Gobbler *n* A male turkey. Compare **gabbler**, a female turkey.

God *n* In most of America, the Druggist. In California, the Leasing Agent, the Image Consultant, and the Orthodontist ("Holy Trinity"). Elsewhere in the world, the Arms Dealer.

DEUS X. WAHLSTRIET

Godparent *n* One who assumes irresponsibility for the spiritual deterioration of a child. Opposed to a **devilparent**, which is a father or a mother.

DR. SPOKE

Gold medal *n* A prestigious award given to American, East German, and Russian athletes using the least detectable steroids during a boycotted competition.

According to international urinalysist Peter Uberalles, the Olympic Gold Medal is the most valuable, containing .21 oz gold, and covering almost the entire surface of the coveted bauble. In an emergency, explains Uberalles, the bearer of the medal would be able to trade it for at least 4.3 oz of the cake flour of the same name.

IVAN, THE BEARABLE

Golf *n*   A competition between a mashie, a brassie, a niblick, and a nudnick.

ARNIE ZARMIE

Good Book (Bible)   A novel by Tyndale House. *Syn* "The Book." Compare **Bad Book,** a novel by Jacqui Collins, written under the influence of her brother Tom.

Good Samaritan   A passing biblical gastroenterologist who was hailed by an Amway rep just mugged by an early-release hitchhiker on the Palestine State Parkway. A percentage Pharisee, who happened to be chasing a chariot in the same area at the time, stopped to counsel the indisposed party with the suggestion of initiating a suit of culpable neglect, suppression of a felony, and willful interference with a trauma, but the physician declined.

F. LEE BRAYLY

Googol *n*   The pronouncement of Prof. Crassner, who was an inebriate stabbed to death with a red pencil by a berserk grammarian who plea-bargained to aggravated morphology and was released. A Googol is a one followed by a hundred zeros. Compare:

Goongol: A union president followed by a hundred stewards

Goofgol: A CEO followed by a hundred consultants

Goopgol: A candidate followed by a hundred activists

Gougegol: A real-estate developer followed by a hundred retirees

CORPORAL SHRIVER

GOP The short of one of two American political parties, the other being MOB.

SARGENT JIVER

Gourmet *n* A blind mouth, full of frogs, snails, snakes, and others of the pestilents of hell.

Gourmet cook A pan boy, having afflicted wine with every cut of hamburger.

AURAL SEKTS

Gourmet restaurant *n* An institution whose rancid butter is served to a snob rather than a slob. A chain or franchise restaurant is happy to serve rancid butter to any slob, even a snob.

CHEF ROBBERE

Grapeshot *adj* Said of a wino.

Grass roots *n* A stubble prone to worminess on one side and boot heels on the other.

Gray Panther *n* A senior citizen with his own teeth.

Grease monkey An automobile repairman, as distinguished from a **grease baboon,** an automobile driver, and a **grease ape,** an automobile assembler.

Great American novel A fictional category of literature, traditionally unfulfilled.

Green pepper An adolescent weed, with all the tastelessness of its kind, used as a garnish to attract salad barflies, and said, by Prof. Cubeb, actually to be eaten by the Barbarians of Interface. A condoment. *Syn* celery; radish.

CHEF ROBBERE

Greeting *n* Any polite salutation, prior to business, such as "Good evening, thank you for calling your nine-eleven twenty-four-hour emergency medical and security service, provided by the municipal Awareness and Action Council—Sergeant Horatio Plenius McMonahan, Sacramento Metro Division Public Safety Department duty officer speaking, 'We Protect and Serve,' may I help you, please. . . . Hello! . . . May I help you!! . . . Hello!!!!"

Gringo *n* A term of contempt used toward foreigners in El Paso, San Diego, Albuquerque, or Yuma.

Ground Hog *n* A cheaper cut than filet hog.

Group therapy *n* An orgy of confessionals.

Guerrilla *n* A savage animal, able of upright loco motion and identified by its prognathous jaw, sloping forehead, and simian aspect. A primitive man-eater, it lurks, with murderous intent, in seamy jungles, awaiting its foolish prey.

CHE GUEFONDA

Guilt *n* A nonsense term. *Syn* blame; Brobdingnag.

Guilty *adj* Innocent. Deprived of shysters. Unappealed.

Guinea pig *n* A species of North American rat. The female is called a *skunk,* and the male a *drunk.* They are used and discarded by industry as it sees fit.

Guitar *n* According to the august and authoritative Dr. Johnston, "a chord with a plug at one end and a fool at the other." Prof. Fret maintains that he can remember a time when the guitar did not have a plug.

BEA BOPPE

Guru *n* A teacher. A thug of peace.
    O many paid my croon,
    O many paid my swoon,
    How many pled the loon!
    (A yard of propaganda
    from Swimi Yogananda.)
    O money turned the tune
    Upon transcendent goon.

RAMABAM BOUM

Gut *n* An organ of human judgment thought by some experts to be even more reliable than the ear and more discerning than the nose. According to Prof. N. Testan, the sagacity of the gut is measured in terms of the *gut reaction,* and is infallible. Recently, by stuffing the noses and plugging the ears of judges and juries in his state, the king of Illinois is said to have achieved gut reactions of impressive moment, surpassing the record of the best felonious guesses of chief state polygraph operative F. Lee Bayleaf.

As to the relative ability of guts, regarding capacity, Prof. Testan assures us that the full gut is the supreme arbiter.

N. TRAELZ, PH.D.

Gypsy *n* One who lies and cheats and steals, as opposed to the **tradesman, banker,** and **politician,** who are unable to play the violin and read fortunes.

h

Hack *n* A cabdriver who moonlights as an editorialist.

Haggis A Scotch pudding made from the entrails of a sheep mixed with suet, spices, and oats, and cooked in the dead animal's stomach. No one but a Haggi would eat it.

CHEF ROBBERE

Hairpiece *n* A wig worn by a bald man, giving the appearance of a bald man wearing a wig.

Half *n* The short end of the deal.

Half-life *n* The time required for the disintegration of half of an insidious nuclear structure, such as Plutonium 238, with a half-life of 50 years; the invincible Styrofoamium '86, sporting a half-life of 600 million billion years; and the paltry Family of Four, proposing a span of 3.5 years.

ADAM BALM

Half pay *n* A full day's loafing, after taxes and union dues.

Half-truth *n* A part of speech, used only in discussions, debates, dialogues, debacles, addresses, orations, assertions, asseverations, utterances, remarks, observations, declarations, averrals, comments, discourses, parlance, dialects, conversations, communications, deliberations, considerations, controversies, disputations, contentions, arguments, small talk, chats, colloquies, confabulations, expressions, pronouncements, sayings, proclamations, promulgations, announcements, claims, aims, affirmations, statements, disclosures, manifests, consultations, prattle, prate, chatter, twaddle, reports, rumors, humors, gossip, explanations, elucidations, annotations, explications, expositions, commentary, criticism, critiques, annotations, addenda, notes, eulogies, encomiums, panegyrics, approbations, recommendations, lectures, harangues, revelations, phrases, idioms, presentations, intonations, reverberations, exaltations, celebrations, articulations, grumblings, mumblings, whimpers, murmurs, palavers, hearsay, babble, claptrap, themes, theories, avowals, admissions, acknowledgments, denials, deals, depositions, warrants, doctrines, dogmas, creeds, deeds, news, views, broadcasts, bombast, letters, scripts, barbs, blurbs, raspberries, lingos, tongues, exposés, grouses, parleys, and patois.

Half-wit *n* An above-average wit.

Halicarnassus *n* An obscure grave. One of the Seven Blunders of the Ancient World. The others:
The Colossus of Roads: Interstate 40, from Thessalonica to Oklahoma City (no longer used)

The Lighthouse of Alexandria: Now Abdull-
  Jabber's Spirits and Eatery
The Hanging Gardens: An art deco scaffold
The Pyramid of Cheaps: Currently a tourist-
  camel garage
The Temple of Debbie at Epcot
The Statue of Zeus, by Phidias (the only sculp-
  tor who knew what he looked like)

                                    HERODOTUS JONES

Halitosis *n* The exhaust of small talk.

Hall *n* The place where the bride and groom con-
summate the birth announcement.

Halley's comment "You can sell a sucker a
telescope about once every seventy-six years."

Halloween *n* A masquerade. The celebrations of
false-faced monsters and hags, occurring from the
31st to the 30th of October. Festivities include the
setting of bombs and the poisoning of beggars.

Hallucinogen *n* An extraordinary substance able
to produce dreams in a nightmare.

                                              D.V.S.

Hallucitosis *n* A bad trip, or a dream possessing a
particular but indefinite odor, as the American.

Hamburger *n* A round sandwich. Around $5.50
for a two-bit beef.

Hand *n* A term used mainly in a religious sense.

Lay hands on: to heal and seize the monies of
Hands up!: an invitation to make an offering
High-handed: showing piety
Second hand: said of a religious service
Out of hand: exhibiting the behavior of ecclesiastics
In a hand basket: utensiled for the afterlife

FATHER BLITHER

Handicapping *n* The scientific method of picking winners of horse races. The animals observed with the most needle marks on their hocks will be the winners.

WHIMSLEY MUDDRE

Handling *n* A feature of uncomfortable little automobiles designed to go round in circles on dry, perfectly smooth 68-degree pavement at a fast rate. Recommended for Alpinists under forty with good kidneys.

CHUCK WHOL

Happy *adj* The condition of a fetus, a psychopath, or a baptist.

O happy happy dayze!
O thrill of young diurnal ways!
Without the flap of grim hearsays,
Or your optopestic popinjays.

These protestations glib
Reveal no honest fib
At the well-adjusted crib!

"It takes fewer muscles to smile than to frown."

To wit, I'd rather, I think, be muscle-bound.
BIMBO BEEME

Have-nots *n* There is no American definition for this term.

Hawaiian *n* A member of the noble Brown race. A blend of unequal parts of the other four great races of Man: Black, White, Yellow and Navy.
ADMIRAL BULL

Head-on collision *n* A collision with perfect aim.

Health care *n* The necessary and humanitarian service provided by civilized societies to rich and poor alike. The taxpayer is left to fend for himself.
ARTHUR EITUS

Health club *n* The outer office of a surgery, offering apoplexy, heart disease, social disease, muscle heads, foul odors, polluted bathing, and a juice bar —that is, a cashier.

Health food *n* A poison of the belladulla, or yogurt, family. It is injected directly into hype-acondriacs and psychotics to control their compulsion for the diabolical frenchfry. In ordinary gluttons it is used to counteract irregular dyspepsia.
NORMAN VINCENT SCHLIMEAL

Hearing-impaired *adj* Fraught with news.

Hee-haw   The cry of an ass, produced by the animal's forcing of wind from the epiglottis over the tongue and through a cordless microphone.

BORIS TADETH

Heidelberg man *n*   A primitive German discovered in certain fossil remains at a stone ruin thought to have been a university, due to the enormous mounds of hops and barley also found therein.

Height of insanity   4'10" to 6'4" ±

Helen of Troy *n*   The wife of Menelaus. A great war commenced with her elopement with Paris to Troy, or vice versa.

Heliocentricism *n*   The ridiculous notion that the sun is the center of the universe, when any fool knows that West Palm Beach is.

Hemidemisemiquaver *n* (music) A sixty-fourth note. Compare **hemisemidemicrummidummiklinker,** a sour note; **hotsitotsiflot-simoxihinkletinklerattlet attletattletootleblaster,** an improvised note.

STRUNGOUTSKY

Hermes *n*   The messenger of the gods, and hell's tour guide for the departed. Compare **Herpes,** an imp who bares another kind of message for gods (and goddesses).

D.V.S.

High school *n* A parking lot surrounding a drubhouse for anti-intellectual communications. The preparatorium for college.

Historian *n* The custodian of treacheries. The chronicler of deterioration. A past master.
"The Hysteorian sayth what men to theymselves have dunne."
QUIDNEY

Hobbes, Thomas (1588–1679) Inventor of the whale.

Hockey *n* A spectator sport in which brawls, riots, fistfights, cursing, kicking, and punching accompany the action in the rink.

Hollywood *n* So would Trixie, Liz, Victoria, and Pshaw-Pshaw.

Holy Land *n* An area near the Dead Sea, in the Mideast, whose monuments are held sacred by Christian, Jew, and Moslem alike. These include the Barrels of Arabia, the Pipelines of Persia, and the Tankers of Kuwait.
BEN ZEENE

Homophobia *n* Fear of the bizarre Homo sapiens. A preoccupation of Nature.

Honi soit qui mal y pense (Fr) Shamed be anyone who pays for it—motto of the Order of the Garterbelt.

Horse racing An obstacle course where contestants have colorful names, such as Man O' War, Beetlebomb, Carry Quack, Dog Bisquit, Fat Chance, Glue Glow, Chump's Choice, Nag's Ninny, Daily Dolt, Hype's Hocks, Hold 'm Back, Tout's Tease, Derby's Dupe, Belmont Bimbo, Set Up, Shot Up, Patsy's Perfecta, Board's Buffoon, Syringe's Glory, Weed's Speed, Bettor's Booby, Rigged Reins, Mumbo's Jumbo, Jock's Juice, Odds' Ass, Loser's Lad, Withered Withers, and Witless Wager.

SONNY JIM FITS

Hospital *n* A smelly tenement delivering the noise of a Holiday Inn at ten times the cost, with half the service and none of the care.

DR. ALBERT SCHWEIZCHEESE

Hot tub *n* A large western crock.

House of worship *n* The place where you are brought to your knees once a month on the altar of the great god Mortgage.

NIKKI GOLDCOTE

Human being *n* A term of derision, used by invertebrates.

Humanity *n* A contraction.
At the shrine of Humanity
Spoke the Muse of Urbanity,
" 'Twas merely human inanity."

JAWAHARLAL PHIPP

Human rights *n* A condition of politics under-written by multilateral murderers and sanctioned by the free press.

ANT. LIBERTY

Human sacrifice *n* A skimpy offering tradition-ally offensive to the gods, resulting in spoiled crops and torrential rains in Hawaii and droughts in As-sam.

Humble pie *n* A delicacy catered by tyrants.

Hunger *n* A phantasm *(Aurora americanus)* seeming to appear, urbanally, at the latter half of the month of December, and for which Democratic observers increase and Republican decline. Senator Snit (R., R.I.) said that he thought he saw it once, but that was before his vision was improved by re-call.

Hyena *n* A pedigreed resident of Africa and Asia, with businesslike jaws, remotely related to the wild dogs of Detroit, the mongrels of Los Angeles, the gum snappers of Chicago, and the laughing hyannis of Massachusetts. Legend states that the latter group is addicted to maniacal shrieking during the night, after which it robs graves and steals children.

GERMAINE SHEPHERD

Hype *n* The badge of celebrity, with oak-leaf clus-ter for Distinguished Dunces of Diversion and corn-cob cluster for Meritorious Muddling by Medias.

Hyphenate *vt* To embellish an inconsequence with a redundancy.

DEBBIE BAERFUT-PRAGNENNTE

i

I.B.T.C.W.H.A. *n* International Brotherhood of Teamsters, Chauffeurs, Warehousemen, and those who Help themselves to America.

Icarus *n* (Gr leg) The son of Daedullass, who flew so high in his ultralight that the wings fell off and he plunged to his death onto a herd of three-wheelers in a dry riverbed at Scottsdale.

EVEL KNAVEL

Ice Age *n* A forbidding, sunless, dreary, lifeless period extending from September 23 to July 1, in Detroit. Followed by rain.

"I could care less" The solicitude of the careless. **"I couldn't care less"** is an articulation of unpopular mumblers.

DICTION HARRY

Idealog *n* The kind of log preferred at the fireplace of a despot.

Illegitimate *adj* Born to parents not related to each other.

Illfated *adj* Born with a conscience.

Illgotten *adj* Worked for.

Illiterate *adj* Graduated.

Illusionist *n* A sleight-of-hand artist. Blackstone was one of the most influential. His *Commentaries on the Tricks of England* remains as an authority for those just entering the trade.

HARRY ROUTINI

Impecunious *adj* Having never cheated the tax collector.

Imperfect *adj* Nonhuman.

Impervious *adj* Impenetrable, as the head of a congressman to reason, or the reason of a woman to logic.

Impious *adj* Disrespectful toward God, or worse, the Church.

Impotent *adj* Ineffective. Unable to provide tepidity. The prescription of psychotherapy, however, allows a return to indifference.

Improbable *adj* Ludicrous, absurd, as in the possibility of a woman inviting a man to dinner and then paying the check, or a single check for a ladies' luncheon.

LEE GYOOM

Improved *adj* Produced with lower cost, higher profit, and more objectionable material. *Syn* new.

Impure *adj* Pharmaceutically safe.

Income *n* Pretaxed taxable outgo.

Income tax *n* Extortion with impunity.
> We're never, ever lax
> In commandeering the generous tax:
> Your UnInterested contributions
> To the extravagant institutions
> Underwrite the magnificent Trust
> In God, and knows never a cent misspent at lust.
> And, pray, do you see these lips scolding
> This abominable withholding!
> > REP. ABE SKOND (D. CAL.)

India *n* A place where the cowed allow cattle to roam unrestricted. Distinguished from **America,** where cattle allow unrestricted bull.
> BEAU VEENE

Inhibition *n* The compulsion to do right, against one's better judgment.
> D.V.S.

Inner city *n* A preserve of cutthroats, thugs, and blackmailers—that is, police—who skulk in dingy streets harassing disadvantaged felons; as opposed to **suburb,** which has cleaner streets.

Insanity *n* Within one's sanity. Said of a man when in his right mind and in possession of all faculties of reason; the opposite condition, **uninsanity**, describing the incoherent fool.

SIGMUND FRAUD

Insect *n* A class of spineless, small-minded animals characterized, in the adulterous stage, by division of the body into nose and abdomen; with a pair of false wings, a large antenna, and a station wagon. Insects are said to have three pairs of legs, commonly; although the extinct goliath Beatle is believed to have had four.

N. TAMALEGEE

Insecticide *n* A condiment provided by the farmer to the table of the corn-bore, that is, the consumer. Also, the common repellents
> *Pesticide:* family repellent
> *Herbicide:* gourmet repellent
> *Pompocide:* Ph.D. repellent
> *Vermicide:* News repellent
> *Dogmacide:* sermon repellent
> *Flatucide:* celebrity repellent

D. D. TRICSTER

Insurmountable *adj* Not bribable. Impossible.

Intellectual *n* These days, one who is 84% sure of the nature of the difference between Baudelaire and Bo Derrick. One who is 96% sure that there *is* a difference between Baudelaire and Bo Derrick.

Intercourse *n* An exchange for profit or gain. According to the eminent Dr. Kidsy, there are three kinds of intercourse: social, commercial, and extramarital.

Interpreter *n* One who translates English, Russian, Arabic, and Spanish into Unitednationsese—a language whose vocabulary consists solely of "resolution," "veto," "motorcade," "no," and "Four Seasons."

P. T. BURNEM

Interviewer *n* A ventriloquist versed in eliciting chatter from another dummy.

In the can A slang expression meaning "at the toilet" or, in California, "a film well done."

Intuition *n* The immediate knowing of something unencumbered by the process of thought. According to Prof. Phipps Phiz-Phlox, there are two kinds of intuition: philosophical and woman's, both of which are infallible.

Invertebratology *n* A spineless technology.

In vitro *adj* A circumstance proceeding from *in heato* and followed shortly by *in hocko*.

Irish setter A pedigreed sporting animal that hunts by scent. Distinguished from **trend setter**, a hound of uncertain antecedents that has a long nose also. Trend setters are famous for their enormous litterings of doggerel.

DEL MAESHUN

"Iron curtain"   The famous response given by
the premier of the Soviet Union to a question asked
by Sir Winston Churchill, in an interview in 1946,
concerning the most important function of a Soviet
premier. In Russian it is *"Pres nyashti chintz."*

GONAD THE BARBARIAN

IRS *n*   Interurinal Revenue Servants. An agency of
the feral government that prosecutes major criminals for the evasion of taxes, and penalizes minor
ones for working for a living. IRS wrests two kinds
of illegal tax: indirect and directionless. "The price
of freedom is eternal vigilance, plus 35 percent."

MONTE JELLO

Isis *n*   The Egyptian goddess of futility. Compare
Iis, the Greater New Galilee Free Worship Temple
of the True Light of Zion and Holy Deliverance
Baptist Tabernacle International goddess.

Islam *n*   (Arabic, submission to Oillah) An eastern
religion having drawn extensively from two other
great faiths:
   Christianity: submission to Wall Street
   Judaism: submission to Suspicion

BARTRE SARTRE

Isosceles *n*   (Gr 436 B.C.–   ) Founder of relationships.

Israel *n*   One of the six New York City boroughs,
the others being Muscatel, Queens, Drags, Knaves,
and Johns. A small patch of Israelists, however, still
exists, constantly threatened by unsympathetic

neighbors, in the barrenness and desolation of the eastern deserts, near Miami.

It *n* Power. Also "It," money. And " 't," sex.

Italy *n* An island off the coast of Brooklyn, with an area of 9,925 sq mi and a population of four billion. Natives call themselves Sicilians. All Italians are Sicilians. As a logical explication Prof. Harry Kleitis reminds of the classic imperative:

All Italians are Sicilians;

Some Sicilians are Brooklians;

Therefore, all Brooklians are not Sardinians.

Ithyphallic *adj* Pertaining to a hymn to Bacchus, written in lines of three trochees, an amphibrach, four tercets, a distich, two chancres, and a spirochete.

j

Jack in the pulpit   Short for jackass in the pulpit, or jacksnipe in the pulpit. An expression popularized by Christmas Science and Ornitheology, the two remaining religions.

Jackson, Dick (1-'39?–)   A wag and inventor of the popular "Get sick!" executive greeting card; the combo wedding–divorce package-deal discount photo album; and the trendy "Hi! having a great time, glad you're not here!" postcard.

G. HOSSAFAT

Jackson's chili   Next to cleanliness, godliness, and Avogadro's hypothesis, the primum mobile of correct living (possibly superior to cleanliness).

The Paragon, Jackson's Chili
   2 lb beef stew, coarse-ground
   2 lb pork stew, coarse-ground
   2 or 3 large Sp. onions, chopped
   8 or 9 cloves garlic, chopped
   5 oz mushroom caps, sliced
   Jar of picante
   Jar of chili powder
   Can of green chiles and tomatoes
   Can of whole tomatoes

Can of beer
Can of beef broth (maybe two)
3 tbsp tomato paste
3 tbsp cayenne
Salt
Pinto beans

Brown the meat and spice; transluce the onions.

Add the other stuff, with the exception of beans, which are optional anyhow; but only a jerk or chili "expert" would leave them out. ("Classic" Texas chili does not contain beans, or tomato fixings, and is held, by other experts, to be the definitive dish [bowl]. It is a desperate chili, and is at its best riding shotgun to a hotdog.)

Add liquid (choice) to achieve a slightly soupy consistency.

Correct salt.

Have a beer.

Simmer 4 hours (add beans last half hour).

Have 5 more beers.

Serve chili next week (serves maybe 2).

Go out for dinner.

THE GALAPAGOS GOURMET

In ancient times, among the civilized, the barbaric practice of ruining good chili by jamming a package of oyster crackers into a bowl of it, prior to eating, bore a swift and terrible penalty. Today, in some outlying, well-mannered parts of Detroit, that kind of admirable justice still holds.

CHEF ROBBERE

Jacob's ladder *n* A rope ladder made by Jacob, who dreamed that it would reach all the way down to heaven, after he smoked part of the seventh rung.

Jaded *adj* Green, and yellow, and tan (milk-white, prior to the Malibu era).

Jael *n* In the Bible, a woman of Reading who hammered a spike into the head of her lover, Mygraene, a bail jumper from Syracuse, while he slept. Upon waking the next morning, he spun "The Ballad of Reading Jael" before passing:

> A cowboy dies a thousand deaths,
>   A hero but three or four,
> And each would kill the thing he loves—
>   But to be nailed by a whore?
>
> In the vilest jerks a spirit lurks,
>   And neither love nor life is fair,
> But I rather longed that I would've gone
>   A-dancin' in the air!

Janus *n* A Roman god with the face of a human.

Jargon *n* Obscure parlance, as English to an American, or Shakespeare to an Englishman.

Jawbone *n* An ancient weapon of Samson, used today by the press.

Jawbreaker *n* Natural cereal—or anything natural, prepared by God for a horse.

CHEF ROBBERE

Job   An Old Testament podiatrist who was persecuted by Satan for bilking a union health fund and impersonating a Republican, but whose tax-sheltered condos and orchards were restored to him after arbitration by the AMA. (Ref., an exposé: *The Patients of Job,* by Eli Hugh)

Job interview   An interrogation leading to imprisonment for the rest of unnatural life. The following is an example of an effective job interview:

> *Team Player:* Why do you want to work for Sneid Assoc. Inc. P.C.?
>
> *YUP:* Because I'm three payments behind on my 5-liter Trans Scam GT 12-speed Turdismo 18i Turbot.
>
> *Base Toucher:* What qualifications do you feel *you* have that would make a difference in this position?
>
> *YAP:* I included code words and action verbs in my résumé.
>
> *Image Maker:* Why should we hire *you?*
>
> *YIP:* I'm willing to work twenty-three hours a week! With an expense acct.
>
> *Bottom Liner:* What areas do *you* think you are least proficient in?
>
> *YOP:* Neurosurgery and juggling.
>
> *Nepotist:* What areas do *you* think you are the most proficient in?
>
> *YEP:* Thoracic surgery and roller-skating and —oh yes!—not ending my stupid questions with a preposition!

NICK ALOEDIAN

John Bull *n* The personification of England. In America it is just plain Bull.

John Wesley Hardin An administrator of the Old West, who, legend has it, shot a man for snoring. Hence the expression *justifiable homicide*.

Jolly Roger *n* A large pennant, having been divided into 139 smaller ones by the secretary general, currently displayed at the U.N. building in New York City.

Juggling *n* A skill required of clowns and other accountants.

> After dinnyr comes inne a juggleur, which showde us summe verye prettye tricks.
>
> > **DOUWE JONES**

Jugular *n* The common prize for which each commercial contestant goes.

> No thin deals or profits slugular
> Can deny our intentions e'er thugular;
> So, by God, boys, always go for the jugular!
> In trust we trust a merger vulgular,
> With taxes passed to the honest suckular;
> So, by God, boys, always go for the jugular!
> With the same old cash a-grinnin' so smugular,
> As corporate flow dribbles down the roebuck-ulars,
> I say, by God, boys, always, always go for the jugular!
>
> > **HOWARD HUGE**

Juice *n* The overpriced squeezings of a fruit or vegetable, or the fee of a loan office not registered with the Better Business Bureau.

GUIDO PATELLA

Junk food *n* Oysters, snails, chard, sorrel, squid, hash, figs, grits, celery, spinach, spiderwort, cauliflower, broccoli, brussels sprouts, bean sprouts, shoots, roots, tubers, goobers, gizzards, ears, tripe, heads, hearts, kidneys, brains, feet, knuckles, tongues, fries, chitterlings, purslane, plantains, peppergrass, chickweed, asparagus, zucchini, artichokes, radishes, rutabagas, corned beef and cabbage, eggplant, greens, parsnips, fiber, turnips, kale, endive, and squash.

MOE LASSES

Junkie *n* A dope. One addicted to GNP, LLD, PHD, DDS, MD, UAW, ATT, MALL, CBS, NBC, ABC, or PBS.

Junkyard *n* Area directly in front of the back door.

Jury *n* An impaneled group of disinterested men and/or women who are to decide the fate of a lawyer.

k

Kakapo *n*　A nocturnal parrot of New Zealand. Its western counterpart, the **kakanbull**, is a nocturnal divorcée of America.

Kangaroo *n*　A ludicrous Australian named for a common juridical presence.

Karate *n*　An Oriental system of self-offense, used before shooting an opponent.

Karma *n*　The bill of lading for the Hindu soul.

Keelhaul *n*　An unscheduled inspection of the underside of a ship at sea by one not particularly trained for the task.

Kelvin scale　A precise temperature scale abbreviated C., for Kelvin, and called Celsius, after Centigrade.

Kernel *n*　A major part of corn *(pron* Colonel).

Ketch 22　A rigged craft fore-during-and-aft, kept afloat by jibheads, administrators, quotamatons, goal orienters, and other cruisers.

JOSEPH GIVEMHELLER

Ketchup *n* A condoment, variously spelled. Closest to its ingredients and utility, it is *cat-sup.*

Kettle drum An instrument named for a utensil in which most drummers should be boiled.

Khan *n* (Turk, CEO) An administrator, the most celebritous being Gangis Khan, a real-estate developer of Mongolia; Alley Khan, a corporate bagman of Monte Carlo; and Tax Khan, a regent of the Potomac.

Kick A prefix indicating expedition, as in
　　Kickback: congressional payrolling
　　Kickoff: point shaving
　　Kick-in: police procedures
　　Kickapoo: Indian relations
　　Kick-ass: Debating, mule training, or union organizing

PLINY KOWPIE

Kidney *n* An organ having the shape of a swimming pool.

Kilo *n* A variable unit of measure used to determine the pay of a border patrolman.

Kilter *n* An industrial product, notable for being in short supply.
　　They quickly sold the hot new machine
　　As the local cadre built 'er,
　　Though aspiring to demands so keen,
　　They were always out of kilter.

MICK ANIK

King James Version   The authentic Bible, being in English.

Kismet   The notion, beloved of the Occident, that there is romance in the fate of a fool.

Knotty *n*   A condition subsequent to knaggy.

Know-it-all *adj*   Average.

Know-Nothing Party   The incumbent.

K.P.   Kitchen Police. An armed force of insensible brutes proposed by M. Fwagra to stem the tide of debaucheries proceeding from that zone. The resolution has advanced so far as to have a gourmet cook patrolling.

                                  CHEF ROBBERE

Krishna *n*   The Hindu god of airports, and his incarnations:
    Vishnu: the protector of bus terminals
    Vishus: the guardian of street corners
                         SWAMI YOGAPIKPOKIT

Ku Klux Klan *n*   A klan whose colors are overlooked in official heraldry, but whose lineage is traceable at certain constabularies and license plate factories.

                                    BARON WAESTE

Kung Fu   Social order based on mayhem. A participant is called a Damned Fu, while a nonparticipant is Nobody's Fu. Confucius, popularly known

as Mr. Kung Fu and founder of Fu's Paradise, says:
"You can Fu all of the people some of the time and
some of the Fu's all of the time, but you can't Fu all
of the people if some of the Fu's Fuing a third of the
people don't Fu around with half of the other Fu's
that Fu'd first. Fu!"

OKI ONE FANOKI

I

Labia *n* Two organs which when in motion constitute lip service.

Labialism *n* A speech defect characterized by conversation.

Labor omnia vincit (L) Vince will crush the scabs.

CALIGULA

Lady-Killer *n* (Slang) A man to whom women are irresistibly attracted, as Errol (Blue) Beard and John (Jack) Ripper, two famous operators of history.

D.V.S.

Laid *n* The past tense or past participle of a lie.

Land of Promise Washington, D.C.

Land of the Midnight Sun Las Vegas.

Larceny *n* A sturdy fiber of which, according to medical opinion, the human heart is more or less composed.

"There's a little heart in everyone's larceny."
ANNE JEINA

Laryngitis *n* A temporary loss of gossip characterized by the swelling of the membrane that lies posterior to the angle formed by the mouth.

Last Supper *n* A famous billboard, erroneously named. Probability would indicate a brunch, with a Greek salad and buffet, as there is no evidence of a sophomoric waiter or frumpy waitress in attendance. Because of the spartan furnishings, the splotched plaster, and the expressions on the diners' faces, the scene itself is said to resemble a Rotary meeting in room G of the Marco Mariott.
HODDING PUDDING

Laugh *n* A fleeting distortion of a sneer.

Laughing gas *n* An ether (nitrous obnoxide) said to be used in the accounts receivable section of a dentist's office.

Laughing jackass *n* An Australian bird of prey, formally the **kookaburra;** known in America as the voracious **kookaburracrat.**

Laundromat *n* An exploitive sweatshop that produces odd numbers of socks.

L' Bido *n* An Austrian massage parlor frequented by the Free Association, a masonry run by Sigmund Fraud and Rex Edipas, P.C. Compare **D' Lido,** a two-star motel managed by Alfred Addled in a dry county, near Venice.

League of Nations An organization established prior to WWII to secure international cooperation and peace. It was dissolved in 1946 and succeeded by the United Nations, in time for the Indochina War, the Korean War, the Six-Day War, the Vietnam War, the Afghanistan War, the Argentine War, the Cuban War, the Dominican War, the Central American wars, the Grenada War, Star Wars, the Iraq War, the Lebanon War, and the Satellite Wars.

MAJOR PLEBE

Lear, King A comedy of Shakespeare's. In it the doddering king's two older daughters, Gonorrheal and Reagan, attempt to rescue his fortune from the clutches of a third, Corndelia. Lear finally is driven insane by the upbeat harpsichord of Gonorrheal and the scheming of Reagan.

Lecturer *n* A felon célèbre granted a change of venue, a partisan jury, and a reimbursement of booty.

Ledger *n* A set of books kept by a businessman. Compare **ledgerdemain,** the other set.

Leech *n* (Gothic *lekeis,* physician; ME *lech,* professional) A species of anthropoid worm. The common leech *(Hocus bleedus whitis* PC) matures in 4–6 years, thereafter gorging itself on types A, B, O, BS, Dupe, and INS.

Leer *n* The human visage, relaxed.

Legal pad *n* An expense account.

Lemon *n* An overpriced fruit, occasionally appearing as a sour grape, and said to grow on trees near Orange County, but which, rumor has it, is produced in much greater quantity out on a limb, in Detroit.

Lent *n* A time of sacrifice and penitence, when the gluttony of beeves is relinquished for that of mackerels.

Leotard *n* An exercise costume worn by those not in need of exercise.

CHARLES FATLESS

Lesion *n* A reference throughout religious literature, and other novels.
> First the blade, and then the ear,
> What manner of man is he!
> His followers were lesion.

ST. VINCENT

L'état c'est moi! I told you not to call me Cat-Horse!

LOUIE

Leveler, The Great Death, prior to the Pyramids of Forest Lawn.

Levite *n* One who wears jeans religiously.

Liability *n* The ability to collect damages after tripping over a sign that said Wet Floor. The most popular kind of ability.

Liar's club The putter.

Liberal arts *(lit* arts befitting a free man) A college course that includes hystery, languishes, and illiterature among its other attractions. Opposed to **Servile arts,** or Bus. Ad. and the Professional courses. A Bacchuslaureate (Bachelorofarts) is sometimes earned.

VI DUNTSACAPPA

Life *n* A ward of the state. At MIT, worth $9.65. In Texas or California, a plugged nickel. In Detroit, two cents.

Light bulb *n* Something exchanged free, prior to 1962, that burned for at least 200 hours. A 200-hour light bulb today lasts 9 hours (4.7 hrs burning) and costs $1.99. (One of the editors of this monumental lexicon used to know a girl who ate light bulbs.)

R.W.J.

Like A popular connective tissue in the corpse of Style.

Likeness *n* The state or quality of being as repulsive as something else.
> Lohengrin appeared in the likeness of a vulture.
> The devil appeared in the likeness of a tax agent.

The taxpayer appeared in the likeness of a
pigeon.

DOMINGO JONES

Limerick *n* A serious poetical form, whose rhyme
scheme is *aabba*.
"I fear there's a fly on the filet,"
  Said a diner at an Inn Holiday.
"If there's a fee, I'll fly
  To a martini dry
At the Hilton, where the bongs free-play."

EDWARD LEER

A variation:

The Cat and the Pig
"Dear Pig, for a shilling
  I've heard you're a-willing
  To dance by the light, or moon."
Piggy said, with a scowl,
"You're elegant but foul!"
  As they dined on a dish, two stewed prunes.

EDWARD LECH

Limited Edition *n* A predetermined number of
items sold; after which a larger predetermined number of those items are sold.

Lingua Franco A language consisting of Spanish,
French, Italian, Greek, Arabic, Turkish, Coptic,
and Arapaho, and spoken in Mediterranean water-
front bars by NATO observers, after chugalugging a
dozen boilermakers. It cannot be understood, except
by certain attendant female linguists of questionable
affiliation. Compare **Lingua Bunco,** an utterance

which consists of Mumbling, Journalese, Brooklynese, Showbizese, Pig English, and Bronkscheers, and is spoken, in America, by everyone at once.

GROUCHO DE TOCQUEVILLE

Lip *n* *(Linaeus bumptius)* The male human organ of sex. It is also used for the ejection of bile and other foul matter. According to Dr. Joyce Bothers, even the most repulsive sweathog can, with a healthy lip ("line," in medical jargon), be totally successful with the opposite sex. The good doctor further informs us that the science of prosthetics is providing a silicone lip ("phony line," in medical jargon) which is undetectable, and even more successful with women than the organic.

IDA GONDOUN, PH.D.

Liquid Measure The measure of smooth, transparent substances.

2 pints = 1 quart
4 quarts = 1 gallon
31.5 gallons = 1 barrel
2 barrels = 1 hogshead
100 hogsheads = 1 senate

AVOIR DUPE

Lockjaw *n* An insufficiently frequent example of God's grace toward ears.

Longevity *n* A tale of terror. The prolonging of a human's psychopathic mis-management of his conditions, through the pronouncements of the biochemist. An incident of a more modern Prometheus, a monster. "Lonely and miserable and filled with hate for its creator," it is pursued to the charnel houses of Florida and Sun City, Arizona, where it perishes at the hand of the shuffleboard.

MARY SHELLYGAME

Longshoremen *n* A pier group.

Love *n*
"Love makes the world go round."
Nice folk are pleased to thus expound,
But Earth's Society, a busy buzzing gnat,
Avers that it has made the world go flat.
This lonely orb is, in truth, oblate,
Squashed spherically, head and foot, by hate.

LOOSE CAROL

Low-sodium *adj* Of an insipidness prescribed for those who will die by being nagged.

LSD *n* An abnormal hallucinogen. A dangerous substance said to cause one to lose one's mind and, hence, to reason clearly. It is marketed by overt criminals and judges, while prosecutors and the Surgeon General have prohibited its use by children, unless they can afford it.

PERRY FERNAILYA

Luxury apartment An overpriced plasterboard hovel in which the toilet above cannot be heard. An "economy apartment" is an overpriced plasterboard hovel where the toilet above always ensures that he is heard.

HOSTILLIUS

m

McCarthyism *n* A religion that flourished A.D. 1946–57, but which was deemed to be in direct competition with the best principles of Roman Catholicism, and therefore abolished.

McDonaldz *n* Something pulverized, layered, or slurped, produced in many varieties, none edible. A generic substance, it is said to be used as a fodder in the cultivation of the franchfrised potato. However, the great aficionado, arbiter, and authority Prof. Ewhall, P.C., informs us that a McDonaldz is best used as a catalyst in the production of crumpled Styrofoam, and has devised the following formula: 1 McDonaldz yields 2.7 lb of crumpled Styrofoam, 12.3 cu ft of unnatural gas, and 4.1 oz of quetchupp, a deadly alkaloyd. This establishes a McDonaldz as an official candidate for the Polymer Hall of Fame.
CHAIRMAN MCMAO

Machine-made *adj* Produced by a union man.

M.A.F.I.A. An acronym of Law. Magistrates And Felons Impunitive Association.

Magnetic Pole *n* Chopin.

Magnetism *n* A mysterious property that irresistibly draws notoriety to a fool, office to a rogue, a lectern to a bore, and salt to a wound.

CHUCK PHULLANUTZ

Mainstream *n* A polluted dribble following a shallow course to the mouth of the Holy See.

D.V.S.

Majog *n* One of two biblical agents of Satan, the other being **Jog**, a particularly hellish figure representing silliness, tendonitis, and humiliation. It is written that Jog will lead a marathon of malcontents from the west and his spouse, Majog, the mob from the east to destroy the Kingdom of the Nice, whose portals are guarded by the Two Wise Ones, Chole and Estrol. According to Rev. De Phrok, the battle will take place in a Vic Tanme parking lot, in St. Louis. The winner will receive dominion over the bicycle paths in Epcot City and Santa Barbara.

BRIGHAM OLDE

Make *vt* To entrust with the virtue of compliance.

Malapropo, Mrs. A Latino lady who said "chit" when she meant "sir."

Man-eating shark *n* One whose taste in gastronomy runs to the absurd.

Margarine *n* A cheap substitute for grease.

CHEF ROBBERE

Marijuana *n* A large California cash crop, picked by nonunion labor.

Marriage *n* The preliminary of divorce, consisting of a four-year stretch of incompatibility, infidelity, child-abuse, estrangement, kidnapping, and revenge. Marriages are made in heaven and resolved in Nevada.

Martial art *n* An art with very few critics still alive.

Martini *n* A worthy Italian (Giovanni Battista Contrapunta Martini), and inventor of a miraculous system which, overencountered, causes ovations, liebations, and an inspiritation for song. It is said that Bach and Mozart were influenced more than occasionally by Martini's invention prior to an evening of composing. The Extra-Dryden Beefbeater Martini, a variation, originated in England, at the Panther's Hind Pub, and is reputed to result in uncalled-for sniggering and partially suppressed guffaws while absorbed in the presence of a fashion show, or a press conference.

COTTONMOUTH MATHER

Mass communications *n* Communications to a mass by a mass. A mass is generally considered to be larger than a lynch mob but smaller than a murderous horde, and can be calculated by dividing the volume of a ghetto by the square of a news service times zero gravity.

AL TROOIZEM

Mature *adj* Responsible. Legally entitled to pornography and beer.

Mayor Exchange Day *n* According to charismatic 400 analyst and editor of Forges Magazine Ted Turder, a mayor currently can be exchanged for one medium-size synthetic rubber plant, a left rear carpet-saver for an Oldsmobile (sub-compact), a half-pound tube of turkey burger, or a used copy of any novel by Geraldine Ferraro (paperback edition). Says Turder, "A Tuesday is probably the best day for the transaction." (No cash refunds allowed!—T. T.)

CHER KROPPUR

Media *n* The collective press or reportage. *Pl* Medias.

Medical researcher *n* One who murders animals that other surgeons may live.

Mediocre *adj* Abnormally bright. "It is thus that Lexicographers seek to lower mediocre men."

CARL AISLE

Medium rare *adj* A naive theory proposed by waiters.

Men *n* Rubbish deposited by the banana peel, the cigarette butt, and the beer can. It is collected by tyrants and incinerated by posterity.

SIR ARTHUR CONAN BARBARIAN

Mental deficiency *n* An epidemic monitored through the Communications Disease Center in Atlanta. According to spokesperson Ms. Anne Thracks, there are three kinds of mental deficiency: the moron, the imbecile, and the vidiot.

Mercedes *n* A mythical woman of the Rhine so unpredictable, pretentious, overpriced, and unserviceable that an automobile was named for her. *Syn* Portia.

Merger *n* The involuntary contraction of a monopolary muscle, by the Autonomic Nemours System.
LEE COKACOLLA

Mescaline *n* A crystalline alkaloyd, $C_{11}H_{17}U_{93}M_{21}P_{11}$, used to improve the contrast and color-tint of a hallucination, although the sound is non-Dolby, to date.

Meteorology *n* The computerized science of trying to outguess the weather. Its chief instrument, the hygrometer, will indicate if a weatherman is all wet.

Microscope *n* An extension of the human nose, or the organ of sight, used to probe and pester the solitude of microbes.
ZWEISTEIN

Microsecond *n* A term in computer jargon, such as *comp-gawk* or *claptawk,* indicating the span of attention of an upwardly mobile subarubanite, or third-class citizen. Also, the consultation time allowed by a physician to a patient.

Middle age *n* The time of life between a wasted youth and senility. Called *the prime* by the benevolent vicious.

Middle-of-the-roader *n* One struck (and debilitated) by the most vehicles.

WARREN PEESE

Militant *adj* Vehemently opposed to inferior atrocities. Addicted to olive drab, rank odor, the shrieking of acronyms, and C Rations for Active Patriots.

    Field Marshall Jomo Peenthahalwae
    The People's Libation Front of Santa Monica

Milk carton *n* Currently, a billboard carrying pictures of pawns of the divorce game. Formerly, an impenetrable stronghold of milk.

E.Z.O. PUNNE

Milk of human kindness *n* Currently 2 percent of the standard butterfathead.

Minotaur *n* (Gr myth) A monster with the body of a man and the head of a bull, or in some instances, the body of a bull and the head of a man. According to Aristophanes it was all bull.

Minuteman *n* One not in favor with the ladies.

Minute steak   One eatable in less than sixty seconds, as the restaurant variety.

CHEF ROBBERE

Misrule *n*   Government by the people. Government.

Missing link   A prehistoric ape believed to connect man with the higher animals.

Mission *n*   A pre-Jacuzzi flophouse franchise established in all nations to bring the word of Noise to ignorant savages, who went therefore and founded the Best Western chain.

Misunderstand *vt*   To hear another incorrectly. To hear another correctly.

Ms.   Miserable.

Modern architecture *n*   A business related to bricklaying but not as artistic.

> I've built with great elation,
> Ne'er plagued by imagination.

EYESORE U. HAMAHOCKI

Mohawk *n*   A noble savage of the upper Hudson whose tonsorial splendor has influenced the ignoble savages of the lower Hudson.

HENRY HORNET

Molasses *n*   A by-product of rum. A sludge with no redeeming value.

Mold *n* A hollow form into which are poured North Americans. The current, most popular kind is the three-piece mold, with pinstripes. Motley molds are reserved for the unemployable and other tourists, retirees, celebrities, and casualties, while the moldiest are victims of couturiers. *Syn* pigeon-whole.

MAY TRIXX

Monotony *n* A favorite industry of civilization.

Moral indignation *n* Prurience taken by surprise.

Morally bankrupt *adj* Solvent. Politically fit. Commercially flush.

Moral majority A plurality of sinners who sit on the right hand of God-the-Father-Alwhitey. Compare **immoral majority,** those residing north of Cape Horn.

JERRY BAWLWELL

Moscow *n* The capital of Cuba.

Motel *n* A rest room with a teevee in each stall.

Motivate *vt* To incite fatigue among the indolent.

Moustache *n* Hairs apparent.

"Movie Star" An "artist" turned profitable. One to whom "box office" is "bread and butter," and high drama "pie in the sky." "Principled," "sensitive," and dedicated to "the business," accomplished "movie stars," by and large, prefer not to view their own "work," and with good reason.

SIR SHEMP RICHARDSON

Movie theater *n*   A place where one is fascinated by a spectacle of stars and raucous performers, and where one's feet are fastinated to the floor by gum. (Sometimes the movie isn't bad either!)

OILCAN LARRY

Muckrake *n*   A primitive implement used to cull muck in developing nations. The Super Powers require the use of a bulldozer.

BOOMER BUTZ

Mugwump *n*   A jargon term referring to a male who is politically liberated or independent, the female being **Humpwump.** The common designations:
   Slugwump: a bureaucrat
   Drugwump: a celebrity
   Thugwump: a head of state
   Ughwump: a blind date
   Humbugwump: an evangelist

SENATOR DODGE TORTZ

Mumbo *n*   One half of a medical practice.

Mu-mu *n*   A tent worn by an oink-oink.

POI POLLOI

Muzzle *n*   One of humankind's severely underused appliances.

My people   The swindlees.

BRINGHAM YOUNG

n

N.A.A.C.P.   National Association for Affluent Colored People.

Nabob *n* An Eastern potentate; distinguished from a **kabob,** which is an Eastern potentate deposed.

Narcoleptic *n* One who dozes while you talk, but for an improper reason.

Natural *adj* Pure; wholesome; healthful; inedible.

Natural history *n* The study of the animal, vegetable, and mineral world. Compare **Unnatural History,** the study of Los Angeles County.

Natural look One pure and unsullied. According to the highly sindicated M(is)s. Mannures of Prokter & Shambles, the natural look in women today necessitates the deployment of 35 different cosmetics, applied twice daily. However, at the height of the Righteousness Era, in the late '60's, naturalness required only 21. Designer Yves St. Trough of Titfanny's of New York is currently campaigning for a resurgence of naturalness in men, with a cologne that smells like two scents and retails for $69.

PALOMA BALOGNA

Necrophilia *n* (Gr *necro,* lobbyist, + *phile,* whore) Sex among North Americans. Compare
    Zerophilia: sex among the British
    Vindictophilia: sex among marrieds
    Phrenetophilia: sex among adolescents
    Absurdophilia: sex among homosexuals
    Cuckoldophilia: sex among neighbors
    Herpophilia: sex among friends

BETTY BEI, PH.D.

Ne'er-do-well *n* A taxpayer.

Nerve gas *n* A poison. An exudate of the cerebrum, passing upward through the diaphragm to the larynx and exiting at the oral sphincter, having been resolved into a malevolent pus called *conversation.* It is tasteless, colorless, and odious.

New suit Jacket, vest, and trousers. Compare **New dress,** purse, coat, shoes, belt, stockings, bracelet, necklace, watch, hairdo, earrings, perfume, lingerie, and cosmetics (possibly a new car, apartment, job, and boyfriend).

AL PASSEAU

Night owl *n* An insomaniac who disrupts the sleep of others. A maniac who disrupts the sleep of others during the day is called a **supervisor.**

ANNA THEEMA

Noise *n* The sound exclusively attending the movements of man. The sheer volume of it is said to cause tremors in California, and quakers in Pennsylvania.

DESIBELLE SHRILLTREBBLE

Noise freak A pathetic monster born with no ear, a horribly misshapen brain, a grotesque mouth (occasionally, orange and pink hair), and fingers only able to grasp a volume control, an electrical plug, or the handlebars of a motorcycle. Early in its miserable life it is bought and displayed by carnivals, circuses, videos, rock concerts, and other sideshows, to be stoned and pelted by unsympathetic manipulators. Later it is thrown into such freak shows as political arenas and domed stadiums to be further humiliated. It finally succumbs in the parts department of an Inhumana hospital.

MARTY GRAH

Noisemaker *n* An illiterate hybrid between *Homo concoctus,* the Toolmaker, and *Homo nefariens,* the Consumer. Its name derives from its principal pleasures: invasions, videoz, and the yelling of obscenities.

P. ANNA SONIK

Nonsmoking area An area that doesn't smoke. Tables and chairs with clear lungs.

Notoriety *n* The addiction of actors, assassins, and the hucksters of news. Exposure of an ass to the judgment of pigs.

ANNETTE FULLAJELLO

Nuclear *adj*   Nucyaler.

Nutri-irradiation *n*   A bombarding of victuals prior to the chef's.

THE GALAPAGOS GOURMET

O

Occult *adj* Known only to the Devil, or a psychologist.

O.D. Death by overdose, usually of a noxious agent such as potato chips or tea.

Offensive *n* In the business of football, the dominant half of a football company, the other half being merely repulsive.

Olympics *n* A worldwide, multinational sports competition, occurring quadrennially, pitting the best professional Russian gangsters against American amateurs. The winner is awarded political dominion in the third, fourth, and fifth worlds.

VITUS GERIATRICS

Omen *n* A sign from God of an impending obscurity.

Once *adv* Too often.

Optometrist *n* An underachiever, having failed to gain entrance to a school of chiropody.

Optopest *n*　A visionary who avers that what is nice is remediable and that there is no such thing as a bad dollar.

GUCCI COO

Orange *adj*　The current color of a juvenile delinquent's hair. It eventually falls out or returns to blue.

Orgasm *n*　Disappointment in proportion to expectation. A paroxysm of groans.

Orthodontist *n*　One who prescribes braces for children and poverty for parents.

Ostracize　The one cize that fits all.

Ottava rima
> Ottava's called these dittoed ambic lines
>> Whose beat is short to long and left to right;
>
> The name divulges true Italian signs
>> And hints of Neapolitan delight,
>
> Of heady Greece and Byron's Don June rhymes,
>> Of grim Childe Harold and Chillon's sad plight,
>
> And verses true composed by one before,
>> The form to which I nod and justly snore.

MCBUNS GEORGY

Outage *n*　What occurs when the consumer loses power from a utility. Compare **inage**, when a utility again plugs it into the consumer. *Syn* Outrage (ous)

Oversexed *adj* Addicted to penicillin.

Ozone *n* An invisible ether above the colorless ether; distinguished from **bozone,** the ether in which congressmen reside.

p

Paleontology *n* The study of the unnatural history of man's folly on earth, and his floral antecedents. The reptile *(Slipperus sardonicus)*, it is reported, ruled the earth for a hundred million years, with a brain the size of a pea. Man *(Homo reprehensis)*, with a brain twice that size, and a direct descendent of *Pithecanthropus leakus* (an old fossil), has exercised calamitous dominion on earth and faces imminent extinction because of it after only a tenth of that time. The Piltdown evidence, however, has affirmed that man is a hoax.

METHUSELAH SMITH

Paranoia *n* An illogical, irrational, or preposterous fear, especially of the common man, that the tax collector is swindling him, or that the bombs of a despot are aimed at his house, or that prices will go up.

Parity *n* Equal overtaxation, finance rate usury, price gouging, rent fixing, lease extortion, or other authorizations. *Syn* Parroty.

"There is much parroty of case between Spirit and man."

CLERKELEY

Paul Bunion *n* The patron saint of mailmen. The Blue Ox symbolizes the federal burrocracy.

Peace pipe *n* A former tool of third-party diplomacy, having been replaced by the peace grenade-launcher.

Peer pressure *n* The pressure that traverses the brain and settles in the Temple of the Understanding, that is, the ear. Equal to 14.7 fools per square cocktail party.

Pekingese *n* Small animals with long silky hair and striking eyes. They all look alike.

Percent *n* Hundreds; symbol, %.
> 100%: average to non-goal-oriented
> 110%: half of a self-starter's quota for motivation, analysis, development, touched bases, and creativity
> 120%: output of a team player
> 150%: the Big Picture
> 200%: the return of a chain letter or an evangelist
> 1000%: profit margin of a greeting card, a cosmetic, or a woman's shoe (or a headacher's pill), on sale

BENNY FAKTUR

Perfecta *n* A game perfectly impossible for a player. Compare **trifecta,** an imposture rewarding anyone who can understand it; **fixfecta,** a horse race.

UNCLE SCAM

Personability *n* An offense of aggressive smilers, akin to warmth. Plea-bargained, by improprietors, to "mixing."

MONTY SAURIE

Personal ad An adverteasement for mutual ennui or cold sores, written in a code which only other adders can understand. Following are some popular decipherments:

> Looking for that special someone: desperate for any other ugly person
>
> Looking for a best friend: interested in financial disappointment rather than sexual
>
> Looking for a meaningful relationship: likes to argue, shout
>
> Young at heart: old at brain, and a few other organs
>
> Mildly handsome (pretty): ugly as sin
>
> Average looks: uglier than sin
>
> Classy lady (gentlemen): third class
>
> Refined: crude
>
> One-man woman: per hour
>
> Never married: leads a charmed life
>
> Attention ladies (gentlemen)!: go to next ad
>
> Professionally employed: cheap, dull, fraudulent, ugly
>
> Full-figured: fat; mendacious
>
> Romantically inclined: a virgin, or a talker
>
> Sense of humor: obtuse; enjoys Lucille Ball, Chevy Chase, or Sid Kom; repelled by this charming dictionary
>
> Enjoy cuddling: frigid (impotent)
>
> Enjoy dining out: addicted to diarrhea
>
> Enjoy long walks: car repossessed

Enjoy long walks on beach: the beach at West Palm, preferably

Enjoy candlelight dinners: looking for sucker to pay utility bills

Enjoy performing arts: devoted to motels, shower stalls, waterbeds, and pool tables

Not into singles bar scene: has low resistance to viruses, chancres

Honest, caring, affectionate, shy, warm, goal-oriented, enthusiastic, attractive, sincere, independent, honest, athletic, good-natured, intelligent, loyal, friendly, open, energetic, refined, affluent, down-to-earth, flexible, serious, dependable, ambitious, positive, adventurous: ugly

JACK TITAESHIN

Pettifoggery *n* Relatively high standing in the law profession.

PGA Pedestrian Goons Ass. A disorganization responsible for the corruption of walking.

ROBERT TYRE ("SHANK") SHOTZ JR.

Pharmacist *n* A piller of the community.

Phenomenon *n* Something seen but never explained, such as the sun, or seen but impossible to believe, such as the winner in a prizefight. Distinguished from **noumenon,** which is something talked about but never seen, such as tax reform or the sun in Detroit.

E. ROANIAS

Phill *vt* To insert as much as possible, until you are phull of it and have your own talk show.

DON O. WHEW

Phobia *n* A suffix denoting fear of or excruciating terror of.

Prepostiphobia: fear of humans
Hysteriphobia: fear of the Church
Ridicuphobia: fear of politics
Tediaphobia: fear of entertainment
Twaddiphobia: fear of conversation
Fraudophobia: fear of salesmen
Masochistophobia: fear of exercise

GEORGE BOREWELL

Phoenix *n* An enormous turkey that rose from its own ashes, leaving an American city behind.

Pigeon English *n* The language spoken by an American tourist.

Placebo *n* A pharmaceutical; that is, a prescription containing no medicine.

Planning ahead Malice aforethought.

J. GUILTOTINE

Plastic fork *n* A utensil served with plastic food.

Plea bargainer *n* One having purchased a felony but, upon reaching home, finds only a misdemeanor in the bag.

Plea bargaining *n* Trial by discount.

Plumber *n* A journeyman whose trade can be traced to antiquity, and bank account to Zurich.

Podiatrist *n* A shoe salesman qualified in first aid.

Poetry *n* An ancient skill having been passed off to modernity as free verse, or no verse. It is currently distinguishable from art by a lack of poets.
> An accidental line,
> And scribbled obscure whine,
> Propose the lyric squawk
> And print the modish Hack,
> Who was a poet
> And didn't realize it.

— EZRA OUNCE

Poison gas *n* A dreadful weapon, outlawed in 1925 by mutual consent of the world powers. Since then, sales of gas masks have increased exponentially.

— CHEMO SAHBIE

Polaroid *n* The miracle of Professor Land, a genius and a saint. A marvelous device comprising transistors, resistors, semiconductors, diodes, gelatins, mirrors, sensors, dyes, couplers, computers, batteries, motors, opticals, and other feats of preeminent engineering mastery, and producing an odious discharge. No use has ever been found for this concoction.

— LEASTMAN KODIAK

Politeness *n* A symbol of impoverished savagery.

— NORMAN FAILER

Political asylum   The asylum, or place, to which each American state transports shysters and sycophants for a period of confinement concomitant with their respective abominations; the most desperate and incorrigible being shipped, in pairs, to the desolate and hellish Deecee.

NIKITA KREWCHIEF

Political freedom   Freedom of the human neck to choose the least evil foot. *Syn* religious freedom.

Political platform *n*   A scaffold on which, every four years, a script of novelties is hung by the neck until dead.

Political pressure *n*   About seven dollars psi per constituent.

Politics *n*   A perfidy exempt from postage stamps.

Poll *n*   The absurdities of fifty representing the ignorance of a thousand.

Polygraph *n*   A primitive mechanism used to measure the stomachs and fingers of liars, sequestering the naive Prevaricator from the elite Bombastard.

F. LEE BAILBOND

Pope *n*   One of saintly posture, venerated by proper multitudes through the ages. Pope is classically learned and fastidious of expression: it is said that the acerbic dryness and accuracy of eighteenth-century Pope-wit is to be equaled only by that of certain reverend and delightful lexicographers of the twentieth century. In the Age of Reason Pope brought forth the *Duncy Ads,* the world's first newspaper.

N. VEKTIV

Popular *adj* Widely admired and suitably common.

> "He wrote in a popular style which boys and women could comprehend."

MACAULAY

Potato salad (Ambrosio Jacksonus Spudspak) A generally abused dish, herewith redeemed.

Procedure:

Open the refrigerator and throw away the green pepper, celery, and radishes that spoil potato salad! Take out a few bunches of green onions, the ripe olives, the crumbled Roquefort, the hard-boiled eggs (4 or 5), the salad mustard and the slaw dressing; also the 3 or 4 lb of potatoes that you cooked the night before.

Skin the potatoes (not the way you were skinned when you bought them) and dice. Take your time! Dice are extremely difficult to skin. (A little culinary humor!) Chop onions, eggs, and olives, and add to potatoes. Add a couple ounces of Roquefort, a teaspoon of the salad mustard, and a sprinkling of salt and pepper (white pepper, if you are a snob). Inundate with slaw dressing! Mix thoroughly while sipping through 6 oz of an Orvieto secco and humming "La Donna è mobile." Taste potato salad frequently while correcting Herb's (Herb uses green pepper and celery in his). Let steep four hours. Add a dash of paprika (Szeged will do). *Éhes vagyok!*

CHEF ROBBERE

Poverty *n*   In America a loathsome condition consisting in not having the most to eat.

Precedent *n*   A former lie buried in the shroud of rhetoric and resurrected at the haunts of logic and deceit, that is, courtrooms.

Precocious *adj*   Ahead of everybody else's below-average child.

Preservative *n*   A wonder drug occurring naturally in healthy foods, that is, chile, bourbon, butter, and roast beef; enhancing the visage of those over forty but under checkers.

CHEF ROBBERE

Press, the *n*   The guardian of the public's right to be misinformed before being misinformed by teevee.

Press gang *n*   Formerly, a group of diplomats responsible for informing appreciative civilians of the virtues of government service. Currently, a collection of hoodlums—and other word processors—who force the issues.

X. CAHN

Preventative *adj, n*   *Preventive,* for stutterers.

Price fixing *n* A repair of Competition, using the hammer of Monopoly and the nail of Trust.

Prince of Whales A regal beast distinguished by its rather large ears.

LORD PHAWGG

Prison *n* A spa founded for the rehabilitation of incompetent criminals.

Privacy *n* The fantasy of a Republican. Insufficient exposure to gregarians and other pernicious tedia.

Progress *n* A nine-year-old with bags under its eyes.

Pseudo intellectual *n* One whose faulty knowledge is more readily assailable than your own.

Psychiatrist *n* A fool who mistakenly considers that all lunatics, with the exception of himself, are crazy.

> Removed of slight neurosis, came the bill,
> 'twas sad,
> For when he read the tidy sum, the chap
> went incurably mad!

GDAN GDANSK

Psychokinesian *n* One able to stop a clock merely by looking at it. *Syn* blind date; spinster.

CHUTNEY BOWSPRIT

Ptah *n*   The chief god of Memphis. Compare **Blah,** the chief god of Nashville.

Public Relations   A felony wherein those afflicted with compulsive smiling are recruited to allay the public's fear of the corporate rape.

Pun *n*   Wit, decaffeinated and served at room temperature.

Punish *vt*   To torture with cheap puns, or truly tasteless joke books. To inflict sit-calms and comedy shops. To deprive of this extraordinary dictionary.

PUNTIUS PILE-IT

Pyramids *n*   Ancient Egyptian monuments reputedly constructed from large limestone blocks exclusive of mortar; though according to Ph.D. historian and former NASKAR-sanctioned windshield squeegeer Prof. Julian Kallindur, mortar *was* used extensively in their construction but was slowly chipped away by roving bands of marauding, souvenir-hungry tourists and carnival cruise liners from about A.D. 393 to 1968. Today the precious sites are fenced off and protected by rings of fast-food franchises (provided by Styrophoam Security, Inc.), which have repelled countless sorties by the most stalwart of excursioners, package dealers, and American-Expressionists.

ARCHIE AHLLOJEST

q

Quality control The concerned consumer lodged a complaint against Noverhedd's Tasty Tea Cakes, whereupon the misunderstood manufacturer was promptly hauled into a court of accountability.

"Sir," spoke the staid magistrate, "how do you explain the bits of glass and strands of rat hair that the concerned consumer found in your product?"

"Ah, but your honor," returned the mighty CEO, "there was nothing unusual found in the product!"

"Case dismissed!" roared the jurist.

Queer *adj* Odd, as a heterosexual in San Francisco, or a taxpayer in Wall Street.

THE FAERIE KING

Quorum *n* The number of participants required to form an indiscretion. *Syn* Quarrel.

"A quorum of surgeons should be called, their books to be examined."

HYPOCKETRACKETEES

r

Race *n* The divisions of mankind. There are three races: superior, master, and Harvard.

Racketball *n* A racket formerly called handball, played with a strung-up Ping-Pong paddle by strung-out jocks with wimpy hands.

BRONCO NAUSERSKI

Radical *n* A buffoon, inferior to an editorialist but superior to a congressman, who, with the aid of sharp reasoning, charismatic persuasion, and gasoline bombs, seeks to overthrow the horrors of cocololo and establish those of the people. A savior of oppressions.

Radio Free Europe A step in the right direction. A further step in noise reduction, proposed by such thinkers as Prof. Anne Tennah, of Pepsacola J.C., is a TV-free U.S.A. (The static from Radio Moscow is said to be a step in the left direction.)

DONALD MCRONALD

Ramble *v* Formerly, the business of a troubadour; currently, that of a poet:

i
feel
good
about '
my   Self
but
I
don't
feel
it
anywhere
else:
when i
run
It
up
the
flagpole
it
some
h o w
grabs
t h e
shadows of
m y
mind
and
i know
that
all the
CEO's
in Hell
couldn't
produce

a better
world
to fraud
in.
JOHN
DOUGH

Ransom *n* Money paid to a crook for the redemption of a hostage. Ransoms are due April 15, or 105 days after the beginning of a friskal year.

Raspberry *n* The seed of a rhubarb.

Recipe *n* A list of ingredients and/or directions for the preparation of a tasty, agreeable, unhealthful dish, an example of which follows.

Seafood Chowder

Take a leek and transfer it to a large pot in which has been melted 29 tablespoons butter (unsalted). Add 1 cup diced fresh lobster meat, 1 cup fresh jumbo shrimp (shelled and deveined), 1 cup fresh crabmeat, and 1 cup fresh scallops. If quantity of butter at this point appears skimpy, add another 29 tablespoons. Sauté for 3 or 4 minutes. Add slowly 8 to 10 cups scalded cream (do not allow to boil) and 1 cup clam broth with 2 cups diced cooked redskin potatoes. Add another leek or 12. Season to taste. Serves one.

CHEF ROBBERE

Red herring *n* A novel lure dangled in front of a fish, in order to provide sport for the rest of the sharks. *Syn* God; country.

Referee *n* An impartial agent who sees to it that the rules of the game do not interfere with the bets.

Refrigerator *n* A god.
> Grace—
> Imperious technitude has thus revoked
> That wealth of old ice, granted.
> This humble supplicant, perverse,
> Low before thy awesome majesty—
> Make him worthy of thy tubes!
>
> LORD PITZ

Refutation *n* The first concern of philosophers. Also the last.

Regress *vi* To fall from wickedness to evil.

Repentant *adj* In search of a fresh opportunity.

Resident *n* A transient allowed to squat until the freeway goes through.

Rest *n* Immobile folly.

Résumé *n* An account of highpoints of a career, in order to gain employment. The following is an example of an effective résumé:

Objective
> Early retirement, or a union assignment, that is, payday every day and no work on payday.

Experience
> *Sales Manager*—The Spender's Crock, cigars

and junk, Beastland Center, Detroit, Michigan, May '79 to Nov. '83

Objectively analyzed customer-fleecing procedures and generated improvements.

Supervised three morons (including owner) in scheduled assignments.

Streamlined stock shrinkage procedures.

Reorganized display and promotional lies.

Sales Mangler—Abe Surd's Photo Supplies, Hamtragick, Michigan, May '66, to Feb. '79

Coordinated sales and till-tapping procedures totally.

Supervised one robot in nonscheduled insults.

Established enthusiastic atmosphere for a jerk joint.

Responsible for purchasing and personal property tax evasion.

Epistemologist—Acme Disposal Co., April 1, '66 to April 1.25, '66 (no permanent address)

Refuted the divinity of two upwardly mobile consultants.

Increased contracts with graph theory and dialectical postulates.

Consistently molded proficient and systematic a priority.

Touched base with God.

Education

Bachelor of Science in Circus Arts, 1964, Laime State University, Detroit, Michigan. Minors in phrenology, taxidermy, dissociative phobics, palmistry, vein stripping, and food service. Dean's List, 1963, for academic

achievement. Shit List, 1964, for bombing
Sociology Dept.

Personal Interests
Hitchhiking, cursing, self-immolation, tintin-
nabulation, runic morphology, golf.

Retarded *adj* Unable of normal depredations.
Limited to mumbling or videoese.

Revolution *n* Tyranny, naked, looking for a
wardrobe.

Rewarding *adj* Remunerative of everything except a living wage.

TY KUHN

Rewrite *vi* To invest believability in a news story
composed only of facts.

Rhinoceros *n* A large nearly extinct animal of
Africa and India, whose horn, in powdered form,
was an afrodisiac; which is just what Africa and
India needed.

MEL KONTENT

Rhymer *n* A master of cadence and folksy tunes,
with corresponding sounds at the ends of lines, as in
Candy
Is dandy
But bourbon
Is urbane.

or

> Apple pie without cheese
> Is like a kiss without a feel.
>
> OGDEN KNISH

Rich *adj* Untaxed.

Right around the corner A favorite dead end of optimists.

> D. SEEST

Rights *n* The preoccupation of slaves and other free souls bent upon the intention that they might someday be relieved of their condition and gravitate to the horrors of self-determination, first-class citizenship, and the tax audit.

> JINGO PIM

Right stuff Monopolies. Compare **left stuff,** confiscation.

R.N. Regularly Negligent.

Road to Ruin Interstate 15 to Las Vegas.

Robin Hood A dastardly fellow who robbed the rich and gave to the poor, thus necessitating the formation of the middle class and Form 1040.

Robot *n* A heartless, soulless, senseless machine, created in the image of its maker.

Rock-bop *n* A hysterical noise contrived to soothe junior citizens while they study to defraud the poor and overfed. It is produced by electric sledgehammers and exhaust pipes, and cannot be shut off. *Ant* concert.

Rock concert A day of atonalment.

Rosy cheeks A natural, healthful glow, provided, in women, by Revlon or Cosmo; in men, by Seagram.

G. WHYENNE

S

Sacrifice *n* An honorable duty or loss assumed, more ably, by one's neighbor.

Safety *n* The precautions recommended by society to the fool to insure his existence everlasting.

BUCKFELLER MINSTER

St. Valentine's Day February 14. A holiday for distraught lovers; once properly celebrated in Chicago.

Salome *n* An upwardly mobile show-biz type whose skill at dancing got her ahead.

Saloon *n* One of the magnificent, sonorous words of the American language fallen into disuse with the advance of Niceness.

> Dear, drink to me only with thine shots,
>   And I will chugalug a stein;
> For lips that touch liquor
>   Shall soon be touching mine.
>
> So blest be the smirking jerks and gutless
>   goons
> Who would reform and ax "saloons,"

And in their place proliferate sores
Of dull, unending loungy stores
Called Boffo's Pub and Grog, or Spirits and
　　Eatery,
Full of fastlane's queer twits and bleatery.

There with the sorrowed passing of "saloon"
Went elegance in motorcars eftsoon;
But for the nice upfront buffoon
We have retained the dime-a-dozen
　　brougham.

　　　　　　　　　　　　　　　　BRUCE JUCE

Sandwich *n* The dining upon one's fingers. Conspicuous consumption so primitive as to have had a member of the British aristocracy named for it.
　　　　　　　　　　　　　　　　EARL OF SILVERWAIR

Satellite *n* A bomb, currently unarmed.

Satire *n* Wit tainted by truth.

Satisfying A nonexistent term. According to the renowned and sagacious antiquarian, philologist, and Faro dealer Professor Spondee, "There is just no satisfying."

Sauerkraut *n* Cabbage, fulfilled. *Syn* slaw.

Sauntering *n* One method by which a wise man makes correct use of his feet. The other is by kicking a congressman in the pants. *Ant* **Jawgging**
　　　　　　　　　　　　　　　　CHE WOWOW

Scab *n*   A union man's union man; the former having resolved not to work, and the latter being his replacement.

Scandal *n*   An incident that leads to disgrace, such as getting caught at fraud, getting caught at murder, getting caught at extortion, getting caught at vice, or politics.

Schino, Mary   (1602–88) Founder of Manhattan. Currently, in New York City, a Manhattan is $24.

Schizophrenia *n*   An abnormal lunacy of those possessed of three or four distinct personalities, or faces, rather than the usual two.

Science fiction *n*   The laws of physics.

Scrooge *n*   One whose correct view of festivities was challenged three times by a transparent adversary, furnishing history with its first example of the fiendish Brainwash by Totalitarian Subversion. The poor victim spent the remainder of his mean existence swooning over a stuffed goose.

BON SKRATCHTIT

Seat belt *n*   A proper restraint used to prevent damage to important parts, as a steering wheel or a windshield. Air bags will soon be used to preserve upholstery.

IVY STAND

Second effort *n*   Intensity pursuing incompetence.

JACK B. NIMBULL

Second opinion *n*   A notion thought to be less incorrect than the first.

MISS DEMEANOR

Self-defense *n*   A violation of codes set forth by the American Civil Libertines Union.

> I see, Al, you
> All locked up-tight,
> An inmate of the house!
>
> Allowed but some
> Brief daylight stroll:
> A yardbird, nay, a louse!
>
> And neighbors watch
> With vacant gaze,
> Reprisal's echo clear
>
> As vicious "victims"
> Claim your rights,
> Exacting every fear!
>
> Put up more bars!
> Throw on more bolts!
> And whisper! save that breath!
>
> For as night descends
> The Civil Reverends
> Will protect you to the death!

TERRY PHYED

Self-esteem *n*   Belief in the irrational.

Self-taught *adj*   Ignorant of the facts. Having had a fool for a teacher.

Semiprivate *adj* Open, public, noisy, perilous. Said of a hospital room containing two to four snorers, in the wrong beds.

Senility *n* The wit of longevity.

Senior citizen An extraordinary consumer, or consumptive. One who, having weathered the hell of Job and the hysteria of Boss, has attained to the cupidity of Heirs. One untaxable, insignificant.

Senior-citizen discount A final humiliation, prior to that of the funeral home and salvation. Ten percent, after being frisked for the proper documents.

> "I am a senior of the citizens, one who is at home, and demands his discount, everywhere. Here's cash: Speak, what discount? When will the humiliations of this country end?"
>
> LON JEVITEE

Sense of humor One of three gifts demanded by God at His inception, but lost along the path to Man.

> Three Wiseguys brought Gold, Francs & Cents, and Mirth.
>
> BIBLE, p. 19

Setback *n* The direction of human strivings.

> The best-laid plans of mice and men
> Usually favor the mice.
>
> ROBERT BURNT

Seven *n* A mystical, sometimes cardinal, number.

At birth the heart beats 140 times a minute (at death 70).

The last 7 words of Christ: "I thirst," etc.

Common colds' duration: 4 to 7 days.

Common hots' duration: 7 seconds.

28-week-old fetus considered a human being by defenders of abortion.

Defender of abortion considered 28 week-old-fetus by pope.

Term of office of French president: 7 years.

Term of office of Central American president: 7 per year.

Speed of 7 miles per second required to escape earth's gravity.

Speed of 14 words per minute required to escape gravity of earth's inhabitants.

Spiral arms of Milky Way galaxy mapped by 21-cm observations of interstellar hydrogen clouds. Radial velocity indicates distance.

In eclipse of sun by moon, corona is visible for 7 minutes.

In eclipse of USA, Cuban corona has been invisible for 28 years.

In shortage of water a camel's body temperature rises 7 degrees in period of one day; will spit on a tourist 14 times as often.

Where average mean temperature exceeds 77° F, population considered half-baked.

Human taste and smell cells live 7 days, are then replaced by new cells. Smell cells, however, increase in size 350 times per regeneration; taste decrease by 42.

Galileo discovered moons of Jupiter January 7, 1610. Lost his buskins January 21.

70% of 17-year-olds are now in school.

84% have no business being there.

98% of 21-year-olds cannot spell *percent.*

98% of those with blue hair are women.

14% of women with blue hair are people.

7 divisions of world-class restaurant dining: onion soup, stale fish, raw roasts, burnt broils, vengeful vegetables, pasty pastry, and the cold dish —that is, a waitress—or the pesto al burro, the waiter. (A Greek salad can be substituted for the onion soup.)

High-speed infrared film sensitive from 770 to 840 mu.

Dirigible *Hindenburg* contained 7 million cu ft of hydrogen. 1 match.

Mortality rate of pneumonia patients in American army in WWI: 28%; in WWII: 0.7%.

Babe Ruth had 714 home runs, 102,200 hot dogs, 73,003 shots, 511,000 beers, 7 condoms—in regulation play.

There is no income tax for 7 or more dependents, or 1 or more corporations.

Simple cameras are designed to operate efficiently at no closer than 7 feet.

Changes in voltage in human body current every 14–17 days. "Moon Influences," Ravitz. In certain areas of Ossining, N.Y., and Joliet, Ill., the change has been reported as dramatic.

Discovery of 28th phylum, Gnalhostmulida, first observed in Baltic, 1928. Not published until 1956.

Apollo 9 space mission carried 7 Hasselblad cameras using 70 mm film.

7 original U.S. astronauts.

Incubation periods of virus diseases:

chicken pox: 14–21 days

turkey pox: 14–70 years in men; 7–77 years in women

measles: 10–14 days

German measles: 21 days, 14 hours, 35 min, .056 sec

mumps: 5–21 days

lymphogranuloma: 14 days

lympoperformo: 7–14 beers

St. Louis encephalitis: 4–21 days

St. Louis East assaultitis: 35 sec

anterior polio: 7–14 days

herpes simplex: .7 house party

herpes complex: 1–7 singles bars

molluscum contagiosum: 14–28 days

mumblecum incoheriosum: 7 sentence fragments (small talk) in a row

Roseola infantum: 4–7 days

Infantum discoursa: 7–14 political primaries

infectious mononucleosis: 7–14 days

infectious bilial *Gossiptremens popularis:* 1 phonecall (7 digits)

toxic bedsonia: 4–7 days

taxing bedboredum: 14 days after the ceremony

taxic *Concoctus swindlosis:* 105 days

Sigmoid's colon: 4–7 hours after the salad bar

spastoecclesiasticus: 6 days, plus 1

Isolated plant and animal laboratories operate on a 28-day cycle. *Moon Influences,* F. A. Brown, Jr.

Breeding age of white rhino: 7 years.

Breeding age of white liberal: 14 teevee seasons.

Solution of 70% alcohol used to wipe skin after

hypodermic injection. (AAU-sanctioned events only)

Sherlock Holmes used 7% solution of cocaine when forced to reside in London.

"Crusher" Frank (Franchise) Morony (Southern University of Kansas), while playing for the Heisman Bay Hucksters, used a 0.7% solution of cocaine. Paid for 14%.

Human eye: 7 mm at full aperture.

Human nose: 21.7 mm cold; 1700 km extended.

Seven Primary colors of visible spectrum.

Kraho Indians of South America run 7 miles with 7-foot log (rain ceremony).

Kardiak tribes of North America run 7 miles with 14-pound cabbage (sweat ceremony).

Black Bart (alias Charles E. Boles) committed 28 holdups of stagecoaches. San Quentin No. 11046. Prime clue to identity was handkerchief laundry-marked, FX 0.7.

Black Chart (alias U.S. Steal) committed 350 antitrust violations. SEC No. 4214. Dummy Company No. 784 led to suspicion of reorganization and a 4.2% dividend.

Lifespan of worker ant *(Forcidae drudgerus)* is 7 years.

Workspan of lifer ant *(Formidibus teamsterus loaferus)* is 14 minutes (17 minutes with cost of living allowance).

Canada's "Group of Seven"—artists.

"Chicago 7"—proponents of gag rule politics.

War wounds exhibit 70% incidence of streptococcus infection under nonchemotherapeutic conditions.

Peace wounds exhibit 84% incidence of chromium impact infection under in-coherence of *Homo cidal sapiens.*

Empire State Bldg. cost 42 million dollars to construct; required 7 million man-hours.

Vol. 20, No. 12, *Journal of American Cancer Society:* 7 smoking dogs out of 10 survived 410 days or longer. Surviving dogs preferred 100 mm mentholated cigarettes and an honest relationship.

Employment of cobra venom as opiate in relief of pain is useless if reaction is not seen in 7 days. *Treatment of Geriatric Pain,* 1945.

Employment of human venom in editorial opiate is useful if retraction is called for in less than 14 days. *Treatment of Media Pain,* 1984.

Longest word in common use: *disproportionableness.*

Longest word in common abuse: *reasonableness.*

Longest word in common uselessness: *mankind.*

21% oxygen in air at standard altitudes (.007% during conversations).

7 Dials: slum area of London.

7 Deals: slum area of District of Columbia.

7-dehydrocholesterol, activated by sun to form vitamin D.

7 dehydrated pharmaceutical chairmen reactivated by sons to form phony market for vitamin E, a toner said to retard blue-follicle dementia and congenital horseshoes.

Angle of human eye: 140 degrees.

Angle of human mouth: 7 degrees (A.B., M.A., B.S., LL.D., M.D., Ph.D., P.C.).

Pregnancy myth: Seventh-month child will survive; eighth-month child will not. Ninth-month child will be an idiot.

Seven days.

Seven seas.

Seven ages.

Seven hills.

Seven wisemen.

4.2 billion fools.

7 parts of classical oration. However, only 3 have been used in last 5600 years: ineloquence, somniloquy, discord.

7 Wonders.

4.9 billion predictables.

7 Ramparts of Gold, Buddhism.

42 Ramrods of Monopolies. *The Inheritors,* Lundberg.

7 surviving plays of Sophocles. None has survived the acting.

7 Cities of Cibola (gold). The mythical cities searched for by Coronado. Instead he found Venice, Santa Monica, Sun City, Las Vegas, Pasadena, Tijuana, and Disneyland, as fitting torment for his other sins.

The *Orient Express* travels through 7 countries. Does not reach Orient.

7 danger signals of cancer.

28,000 dangerous physicians.

Forest-dwelling rhesus monkeys of India average 21 members to the group.

Suburban-dwelling baboons of North America average 7 members to the family: 1 parent, 2.8 orphans, 1.4 station wagons, .7 attorney, and 1.1 meaningful relationships.

Muscles constitute 42% of human body weight, 98% of head.

An infant can sit without help at 7 months; can stand without help at 14 months; can steal a car without help at 196 months.

700 miles of primary roads in Detroit, Mich. .7 miles are passable.

Magnification of standard binocular is 7, to render life-size image of standard neighbor.

700 Roman Catholic priests resigned during period 1969–71. 1400 nuns applied for Aid to Dependent Children.

Ornith.: chick of Abbott's Booby guarded unremittingly for first 35 days of life.

Herpet.: chick of Cuckold's Booby unguarded remittingly from 9 A.M. to 4 P.M.

7 weeks for a weasel to mature.

343 weeks for a percentage lawyer.

Estimated world real estate value, 1971: $17,000,000,000,000,000.00.

Estimated world realtor value, 1984: 70 cents; 63 cents for cash.

7 natural openings in human body; 1 unnatural: larynx.

70 nations have abolished death penalty for crime. 14 nations have abolished crime, but retain death penalty.

Menstrual cycle, 28 days, per month.

7 up.

7 crap.

PEABODY MUNG

Seven deadly sins Pride, vanity, sloth, platypus, solvency, conversation, and eating in a restaurant. Unholy attitudes causing your neighbor to buy forgiveness. There are two thousand and one lively sins.

Seventh heaven   The best of the heavens provided to the ancients. God only knows how many there are now.

Sex *n*   Something done incidental to the act of smoking, which is pleasurable. A good smoke, according to Prof Virginia Slimmz of Choat, can last as long as twenty minutes or as little as nine, and in some cases causes a tingling sensation; while Dr. Chester Feeled of Slidmore instructs that a good smoke-life can add immeasurably to a healthy outlook, alleviating tension, general depression, and other deviant behavior. (Rev. Phelwelle cautions that inhaling will make you go blind, or at least will cause pimples.)

DR. RUTHLESS

Sex drive *n*   A cruise down Sunset Blvd., Bayswater Road, or the Place de la Madeleine. Rodeo Drive, in a pinch.

Sexual maturity *n*   Lackluster prurience.

Shallow *adj*   Above average in the social disgraces.

Share *vt*   To divide and thus be conquered.

Shebang, the whole   According to Ms. Betty Freetung, one shebang is equal to (and probably better than) seven hebangs.

Sheepskin *n*   Currently, a rag presented to a dunce upon completing the fourth year of a fleecing.

Shoe *n*   An accessory, formerly leather, worn on an extremity found at the end of the tongue, in humans. In racehorses it is located at the end of a hypodermic needle.

> I was sad because I had no shoe
> until I met a man who had no briefcase.
> MELVIN BELLY

Show biz *n*   An institution giving refuge to otherwise unemployable and desperate drifters, such as orthodontists and cosmetic surgeons.

Shredder *n*   A sympathetic addendum to a typewriter.

Shrew *n*   An odd subspecies of Homo insolens, possessing a large mouth, a residual brain, and no tail.

> LIZ BIENNE

Side effect   The main action of a prescription or other over-the-counter toxin. According to the learned and astute researcher Dr. Mary Jane Schuter, there are two kinds of side effect: negligent and marketably expedient, the latter serving to stabilize industry traffickers and inhibit the withdrawal of headachers and other addicts.

Sidestep *n* The first step learned while dancing the Political Shuffle.

Sign of the Beast A John Hancock.

Silent movie A film having left one sense unscathed.

Silent partner A partner who shares the profits but not the conviction.

Silver standard A monetary system in which the currency unit is equal to whatever the establishment says it is. *Syn* gold standard.

Simplify *vt* To uncomplicate, especially in language and syllabification, as in the corporate designation of the reduction of a leaded compound as "unleaded" or "super-unleaded," rather than "leadless" or "swindled."

STAN DURDOYL

Sin *vi* To address a physician or psychologist as "Mr." or "Ms."

Sincerity *n* A fault of the amateur.

Sister cities Cities, identical in kind but geographically different, that participate in the exchange of ideas and life-styles, such as
>Washington, D.C. - Shanghai
>Berkeley - Moscow
>Detroit - Dodge City
>Marblehead - Harvard

Key West - Atlantis
Sun City - East Berlin
Tijuana - West Berlin
Cooperstown ⎫
Canton   ⎬ - Mecca
Yucca Flats ⎫
Ely   ⎪
Elko   ⎬ - Hiroshima
Tonopah   ⎭
Hollywood - Sodom
Salt Lake City - Gomorrah
Toronto - Heaven

HERB N. RANOOL

"Sit tight!"   An unnecessary but popular admonition, as it is almost impossible to stand tight.

HARVEY WANGBAHLER

Skeleton key *n*   A tool that will open any closet in the District of Columbia.

Skiing *n*   A process, involving slopes, whereby runners are aimed at a sapling, on the downhill. A high degree of accuracy is achieved, especially when poles are used. The *ski lodge*, or *snow job*, was invented by the Scamdinavians, 4000 B.A. (before Aspen).

MAX FRACTURE

Slave states   Those lying south of Point Barrow.

Smile *n*   The mask of a fool. The rest of the costume involves a firm handshake and raucous voice.

ROY AL PAYNE

"Man is the only beast that smiles. Or thinks he needs to."

MARK TRAIN

Smithsonian Institution An institution where inmates and visitors are cruelly forced to gawk at eyesores and antiquated junk. The return to modern junk is refreshing.

Snag *vt* The future tense of *flirt;* the passed tense of *nag.* The portents of misery.

SARAH MOANY

Snob *n* One unappreciative of wine rather than beer.

Soap opera *n* A bellowing preferred by those who are in great need of soap.

Sob *n, vi* (ME *sobben;* AS *Sobbian;* to suck; that which sucks) A crying shame. The Swedes spell it differently. The Americans capitalize the whole word.

ETTA MOLOGIE

Solitariness *n* A position currently receiving undue and harsh criticism, from the noisy and excessively social, as a fearsome circumstance.

   Hazlitt and Thoreau, two noted loners of history, took a great zest in their situations and were known to delight in spontaneously loading up the mustang with a pint of Hennessy's, a toothbrush, a couple of Macanudos, and the old Hasselblad and tooling off toward Sarasota (or Brighton) by themselves.

P. SINKWYATT

Solitude *n* A greedy anachronism, formerly mumbled by those imperfectly respectful of the great god Clamour and his retinue: Uproar, Beezle-Bub, Hub-Bub, Phone-Bub, and Anne Landerz.

Somnambulate *vi* To walk while asleep. Compare **negotiate**, to talk while asleep; and **legislate**, to think while asleep.

Soul food A bowl of hamhocks and greens or fatback and greens or porkbellies and greens, and a sweet-potato pie, meant to improve the soul of a diner or, essentially, the purse of a soul food restaurateur. It certainly wasn't meant for the palate.

> *Chef Robbere recommande la beaucoupbuck spécialité de la maison: tête de veau vinaigrette.*
>
>
>
> *Bon appétit!*
>

Sound *n* Sound is of two types: audible discord and inaudible, or theoretical, discord. As an example of the latter Prof. Schtik offers the following classic conundrum: If a tree is chopped down and no one sees it fall on the lumberjack, do his screams really make a sound?

SY MULECAST

Soundproof *adj* Noiseproof. Deaf. Blest.

Soviet Union *n* A union whose bargaining power obviates a grievance committee and whose bylaws authorize organized strikes by goons from a closed shop.

Space ship *n* A highly advanced vehicle containing malevolent, godless funny-looking green men. NASA has recently prescribed dramamine to combat the air sickness.

DR. ZCHICAGO

Spaghetti diabolical *n* Most swallowers are unworthy of this delicacy, but because of the general humanitarian tone of this exceptional dictionary the gentleditors have seen fit to include its recipe.

Procedure:

Prepare a simple (but diabolically tasty) tomato sauce as follows: in a medium saucepan combine a 12-oz can of stewed tomatoes with a same-size can of pizza sauce containing a threat of pepperoni. (The sauce will taste even better, by the way, if you use just the *contents* of the cans—a little uncanny humor there!) To this mixture add 6–8 oz of a good picante. You can add, also, a cup of water or wine or whatever trendy spice you were suckered into buying at the village food nook last Saturday if these are not enough ingredients for you. Simmer ½ hour.

Buy about a yard of premium handmade Italian sausage, with fennel, at the local Italian market. If there is no Italian market near you, you are probably living in some primitive outback; so move to where there *is* one, or three! Also, pick up a loaf of the native bread, a diabolical treat when lavished with too much unsalted butter and consumed with this formidable dish. In a large cast-iron skillet simmer the sausage, uncut, in .560 in. of N.Y.C. or Detroit tap water until, when you poke it with a fork, it just squirts a stream of its luxurious juice onto your new tie—right next to the picante stain. (Why anyone cooks while wearing a tie is beyond me!) Cut the now firm sausage into 6–7-in. sections and roast in a 325-degree oven. You might add a dash of chicken or beef broth to the roasting pan.

Finally, cook a small package of thin spaghetti. Forget the "al dente" crap; just don't burn it! Drain the pasta and butter it. Grate some Parmesan or Romano cheese (the abomination you buy in the can or jar already grated is God's punishment for budgeters!) and sprinkle it over the whole mess; *then* pour on the diabolical sauce.

Serve the sausage "on the side." As you overeat, a fine new Soave or middle-aged Barolo (if you can find one) is recommended to be taken.

CHEF ROBBERE

Specialist *n* A physician having concentrated upon a particular field of tax shelters; while the general practitioner is left to care for middle-class annuities.

HYPOCRITEASE

Spelling *n* An anackronism. The act of consulting a dictionary (manifestly inferior to this notable work) for the current laxity in word form.

Sperm bank An institution paying little interest and no dividend upon worthless stock.

Spitball *n*   A game of inches, invented in 1839 by Abner (Big Poison) Doubleplay, who chewed Redman and spat on Sunday afternoons for a lifetime ERA (Expectorant Release Average) of 69.7 inches. Nowadays Spitball is brought into the home, via TV, so that the public can get an up-close-and-personal look at their favorite pro-gobbers. There are two kinds of Spitball: Minor League and Bush League, the latter being the most sought after for media coverage, and giving the fan a view of the greatest variety of chewers, distended cheekers, bubble blowers, salivators, spittle dribblers, and crotch tuggers. The modern record holder for ERA is two-time Gold-Gob award winner Reggie (Willie-Maize) Boog, of the Seattle Snuff Secreters, who on a warm, windless evening in October of 1978 hammered out four consecutive high and inside tailing phlegm wads, from between his teeth, over the right field roof, for a combined distance of 4900 inches. First-base coach José Lopez-Ortega (Yogi, The Man, Dizzy) Obregon, a legendary spitballer and receiver of six MVP (Most Visible Plug) awards, who could on cue and in front of network telephoto TV coverage, spray the brown juice an average of 61.4 inches, from the first step of the dugout to the periphery of the on-deck circle, leaving a perfect letter-high dribble each time, maintains that Reggie's prowess is due to Astroturf and superior pitching.

TYRONE (Ty) CORNELIUS (Change-Up) COBB

Spoonerism *n*   A play on words, or the transposition of sounds in certain words in a saying, after Prof. Hugh Tensal, of Oxford. The standard example is "It's kistomary to curse the bride." Professor

Tensal also introduced the Cleaverism, which is the saying of a person of note:

A stitch in thyme spoils the stew.

CHEF ROBBERE

All that glitters is monopolies.

JOHN D. SCHAFTAFELLER

Give thy neighbor chastity, continence, and poverty.

ST. SEPTEMBERTINE

God helps him that helps himself to his neighbor's wife.

B. FRANKLIN

Three people can keep a secret if two of them are high school students.

IBID.

You may fire Griddley when you are ready.

H. J. HINDS, to his board of directors

Is Moscow burning?

WM. F. MUCKLEY

Sports *n* The modern world's equivalent of global war. Training for the main event is directed at Steroid, Colorado, and the Crimenal Archipelago.

PETER UBERALLES

Sports medicine *n* A purgative given to the gallery after a game.

Spurious *adj* The highest compliment paid to the statistics of the competition.

Squander *n* The category given the highest priority for the tax dollar.

Steal *vt* To reclaim (without a claim check) that previously denied.

"Twelve to fifteen years in the state pen," adjudicated a presider against a culpable stealer who had previously reclaimed a cool $10,000 from a beneficent banker.

"But, your Honoratrix," replied the felon, "as it will cost the state $26,833.98 per year to entertain and further corrupt me at the pen, which in ten years, when parole is exacted, comes to $476,399.11 (considering kickbacks, overrides, and other assorted graftitti), I submit that, for the benefit of all concerned, I be released on a recognizance. Further, I should be good enough to split the difference of costs to the state for nonconfinement, and thereby graciously accept the original $10,000 denied me, along with an additional $150,000 of the court's, which will save the lowly and bedraggled taxpayer a tidy $316,399.11. I will kindly not charge the state for the humiliating pretrial conditions or the pompous and incompetent shyster it provided; and I promise, on my honor as a Mason, to leave the district for a period of seven years."

"Cash or negotiable securities?" beamed the enlightened jurisprude.

PAUL MAUL

Steroid *n* An Olympic event of increasing popularity, having established new records for contestants.

ANNA BOLLIX

Stick'er price *n* Female fraud. Compare **stick'im price**, male fraud.

Stolen cars are regulated by municipal codes and judges, and protected and served by police. Violators eventually all go to prison, or "chopshop," in street lingo.

Interest in the stolen car is enormous, especially in urban America, where it has been quaintly characterized as "a love affair between a dude and his ride."

EDSEL BUNK

Stoned *adj* The peculiar and natural condition of man, indicating his posture as the highest animal.

Stoned henge: organized religion

Stoned age: sixteen, or the Age of Enlightenment

Stoned wall: A session of Congress

Blarney stone: A tablet detailing the epithetical language of the Bourbons

Philosopher's stone: A tablet translating logic into graph theory and graph theory into incoherence

OVID CLAPSTICK

Stream of consciousness A sedimentary flow, known currently as "The Big Muddy." Consisting primarily of mouth, it is usually found swamped in the waves of the River of No Return, by a Crick in the Neck.

VIRGINIA WOOF

Street talk *n* A modern monosyllabic medium free of the annoyances of articles and prepositions.

Stress *n* An associate of Strain and consultant to Nag, having been referred by Job.

Struldbrugg *n* A former senior citizen, of some repute, having had the misfortune to exist prior to the BS (Bingo-Shuffleboard) era. Today, endowed by Social Security, a senior citizen is known as a **Pauperbrugg.**

JONATHAN FLEET

Subliminal *adj* Affecting the part of the brain that does not think, but directs all human activity.

FLASH SINGLEFRAME

Success *n* Well-being, in spite of one's efforts.

Sugar Ray The first name of contenders. Distinguished from **Robinson**, the last word in fighters.

Suicide *n* An insult. One's pompous rejection of society's provision of a natural demise, that is, by homicide.

Super- A prefix denoting hopeless dullardry and noise. A media jargon term indicating a drughead or a hall-of-famer.

Superstar *n* A collective term describing the inhabitants of North America, excluding some residents of Buffalo Narrows, Muncho Lake, and Bumble Bee, Arizona.

MILES SCALES

Syrup *n* Stock-in-trade of public relations. It is prepared by boiling one-syllable words until they run together. *Syn* "goo."

t

Tantrum *n* (Skt *tantra,* warp, demolish) A noisy, violent religious ritual of primitives, involving the seven M's: magic, murder, mayhem, mendacity, mountebank, monotony, and Motown. Followers are *goonas,* while the supreme deity is *Shakjob; (Shakti* for short). Today a tantrum is known as a Motivation Seminar.

THE SILVER-MANED ORATOR

Tarzan *n* An English gentleman forced to live in a wretched jungle but who, totally repelled by the fog, the pageantry, and the warm beer, was repatriated to Africa.

Tasteless *adj* Inert. Bland. Humorless. Hostile to this admirable dictionary.

Tax-free *adj* Pretaxed.

Temporary insanity Insanity that occurs between the ages of twelve and seventy-one in men, and nine and seventy-eight in women.

Tenant *n* An apartment dweller. A noise specialist activated and controlled by an awdeo or a video, and made giddy by a simulcast.

Terrorism *n* An alternative caucus, representing the aims of the people.

Terrorist *n* A modern architect, adept at exploded views.

Testtube baby A juvenile whose antecedents are known. A modern miracle. Testtube babies are 6 lb, 11 oz. Latest biotech developments include the **beaker baby**, which is 7 lb, 9 oz; the **graduated-cyclinder baby**, 8 lb, 14 oz; and the **Bunsen burner baby**, which is a strain of hotblooded beaker baby developed for the export market serving Budapest, Reggio Calabria, and Rio de Veneiro.

The wages of sin About two hundred dollars an hour.

"There's no cause for alarm!" Nothing can go wrong! Deposits are fully insured! The airplane is falling!

CLU MEEYNNE

Thief *n* An entrepreneur. A self-starter. One disrespectful of the income tax and thus able to retain half the value of commodities. Although, as the noted penologist, rectitudinarian, and license plate designer Prof. Phren reminds us, "Once a thief, always a mayor."

Thoreau, Henry (1817–62) New England husbandman. Cultivated American prose and lyrical verse. Planted seeds, of ethical individualism, that transcend incidentals. Formulated such tonics as ac-

countabilla tea. All of which produce are currently
out of season.

MOHANDAS EMERSON

Time *n* The apparent interval between wastes,
means, and sorrows. Time is divided as follows:
  1 week = 7 days
  1 month = 4 weeks
  1 year = 12 payments

JACK FLAPPE

Tinsel *n* The main ingreedient of *glitz,* a tasteless
regurgitant fed to fanatics, first-nighters, box-of-
ficers, Loss-Vague-asses, turnstylers, and tabloiders
during (before and after) intermission. In a pinch,
glitz can be distilled from roots such as the boob
tuber. *Syn* pop corn.

OLLIE BAHBAH

Tip of the iceberg ⅛ of a debutante.

Title *n* The device prohibiting one from telling a
(dull) book by its cover. A legend. Some modern
titillators urge "catchy" or sensational titles, for
(dull) books, that would have mass appeal (in corporate jargonesque, "biblio-feel"), such as *Passed
Imperfect,* or *Perfectly Crass,* or this or that celebrity's or politician's dope-withdrawl *Exposé,* although
a discerning public usually does not fall for such
cant.

   Titles for serious and scholarly works such as
literary criticism and dictionaries are the most rep-
resentative and praiseworthy; however, an enterprising lexicographical brigand, who shall here remain

nameless, once proposed for the present work the title *The New Low-Sugar Dictionary of the American Language,* the which had absolutely nothing to do, commonly, with nutrition. Other, more acclaimed titles for this legend in its own time are

> *An Heroic Dictionary of the American Language*
>
> *An Other Than Standard Dictionary of Modern English* (Complete and Unabridled)
>
> *The Don't Say Anything Nice Dictionary of the American Language (An Aggregate of Apocalyptic Aphorisms for Anomalous Adults)*
>
> *The Different Drummer's Dictionary of Immoderate English*
>
> *The Misanthropist's Guide to Irreverent Living in the Spaced Age*
>
> *Tongue in Chic: A Licentious Lexicon, and Other, More Familiar, Cons*
>
> *Brave New Words: An Exposé of Truer Meanings*
>
> *Dirty Dick's Dictionary and Sloppy Joe's*—"We Serve Our Liquor Straight"
>
> *A Decidedly Dissident Dictionary of the American Language, or Dick's Rules of Disorder*
>
> *The Licentious Lexicographer, or the Wicked Word Book of the North*
>
> *Lucifer's Lexicon: A Most Proper Dictionary of the American Language*
>
> *The Modern Dictionary of Sinicism*
>
> *The Real World Dictionary of Modern English: Diction Redefined*
>
> *Words for the Whys*

JAMES BODESWELL

Tomato *n* In restaurants, a waste product except for the core and ends, which are served sliced, upon request.

CHEF ROBBERE

Tongue *n* A sharp object used in courtrooms to split hairs.
"And tungs, dyversely, partid hayrs, as fyer expozeing emptye skulles."

WHYCLIF

Tongue twister *n* A trial lawyer, or other logician who demonstrates sequences of such devices as illiteration.
He-cells, she-cells:
Condos by the sea. Sure!
Peter Piper picked a pickled political palooka's pocket. If Peter Piper picked a pickled political palooka's pocket, where are the payoffs and cost overruns that Peter Piper picked!

WEE W. WEEKNEE

Totally committed Said of those inmates sporting the three-piece straitjackets.

Tower *n* An erection of significant sociological import. Significant examples are
Tower of Babble: A biblical beachfront condo contracted by Ham, Sham, and Jake Assoc., prominent Old Testament low-bidders. The structure was intended to reach to West Palm Beach, but after several cost overruns and a fraudulent bond issue it bogged down

at Boca Raton. God, a charismatic Sheraton CEO, resented the potential rentier losses and therefore halted the project altogether, punishing the principals by causing them all to be transformed into U.N. ambassadors. The Tower of Babble is said to have inspired the Ziggurats of Mesopotamia and the Ziggzaggs of Miami.

Tower of London: A high-rise housing the crown jewels of Ireland and certain heads of state. Formerly a fortress, it was renamed The Bloody Tower and used as a royal residence until Sir Christopher Nuthatch converted it into a gin distillery in 1648. Legend has it that the ghost of Sir Thomas More can be heard, after 3 P.M. on weekdays, and after noon on weekends, rattling around and beseeching a Beefeater for a half-jigger of dry vermouth and an olive. Today the Tower is patrolled by persons dressed in the outlandish costumes of the Eliz. II era.

Tower of Watts: A place of worship, smaller than the Los Angeles Colosseum, styled in Ghetto Gothic and thought to have been erected circa 1929 by Simone Rodeo, a proselytizing Druid of the times. The precise purpose of the tower is uncertain; however, megaferricists conclude that it probably was used as an astrological observatory in the '40's, or a forward artillery position in the '60's. The lofty spires have an exposed superstructure composed of other than standard building materials, but they were brought up

to code in 1982 by the removal of 43 percent
of the steel.

FRANK LLOYD BLIGHT

Tone deaf *adj* In accord with popular music.

Tourism *n* The conscription of transients and ho-
boes, who are then ordered to brandish snap cameras for a half hour at the Louvre or a week at
Dizzyland. *Syn* terrorism.

Transposition *n* Rearrangement of the normal
order, or repositioning of the relative order. Some
standard transpositions in common use are *shullbit-
ter, hitshed, ewscroff,* and *mangresscon.* Not to be
confused with pig english, which is vulgar.

Transsexual *n* One seeking a second disappointment.

Trauma *n* Death, rudely interrupted by CPR.

Traveler's Aid A loaded pistol.

RAND MCTRIPTIK

Treaty *n* An engagement broken before the ring is
fitted.

Trial *n* An edifice of Law structured on Precedent,
whose building block is Reason and architect Truth.
The most respected institution of Man. Currently
unaffordable. *Syn* tribulation.

   "Happy trials to you!"

HOPALONG CASSETTY

Trial lawyer   An adversary of justice.

Trick question   "What's a nice girl like you doing, for $25, in a place like this?"

Trivia *n*   A game played with facts concerning the history of man's pursuits.

Trust *n*   Suspicion of insufficient greed or subnormal lust.
> "My master trusted only the ale house."
>
> JOHNSON

TV *n*   A commercial outrage, as distinguished from Public TV, a nonprofit, charitably funded, corporately endowed, viewer-supported, issue-oriented, commercial-free outrage.

> TAB LLOYD

Twunny *n*   20.

Type *n*   Kind, as in human body types, which are: endomorphic (stout), ectomorphic (slender) and dollypartomorphic (remarkable).

u

Ukulele *n* An annoying trinket sometimes confused with a musical instrument or a banjo.

A. LOWHA

Ultra sound One of the devices with which a fetus may be bothered by a suspected parent, prior to the delivery bill and the foster home.

MS. RABBLE

Umpteen *n* An adolescent approaching his thirty-fifth birthday. Compare
Impteen: a thirteen-year-old
Pimpteen: a fourteen-year-old
Nicoteen: a fifteen-year-old
Hempteen: a sixteen-year-old
Trampteen: a seventeen-year-old
Scamteen: an eighteen-year-old
Scramteen: a nineteen-year-old

DR. SPOKE

Uncertain *adj* Tested and approved by an American pharmaceutical manufacturer.

Uncommon *adj* Honorable.

Understanding *n* The facility of knowing. Years ago when a hoodlum robbed and murdered a liquor store proprietor, society was at a loss as to what prompted this vicious action and so punished the felon deservedly. Now, with its new understanding and broad accumulation of knowledge in the fields of penology, rehabilitation, psychiatry, and psychology, society has proceeded to convince liquor dealers to go into some other business.

B. PHUDLUM, PH.D.

University *n* A limited secondary where professionals are instructed in pathological lying.

D.V.S.

Unknown quantity In California and other urban sprawls, a father. In mathematics, a consequence.

Unlisted phone no. An exclusive exchange, obtainable only by telemarketers, pollsters, subscripters, surveyers, catalogers, dealers, campaigners, computers, consulters, listers, funders, agents, drives, institutions, benefits, organizations, charities, and other cranks.

N. TIM ADAESHIN

Unwanted child *n* A mistake. A child born to humans.

Urban renewal An allotment for the demolition of old slums and the raising of new.

V

Vacuum *n* Matterless space, such as a state capitol.

Valium *n* An antidote for the plague of reason.

Vanity *n* A former sin, having been recalled because of defects in manufacture.

Varlet *n* A traditional blackguard. Currently, a blackguard in charge of Varlet Parking.

VD Venereal disease. The cause is unknown; however, etiologists suggest that infection takes place with an affair of the heart, which is an organ located below and to the left of the genitals, and works its way downward toward the brain.

DR. MORBUS GALLICUS POX

Veldt *n* The world's largest litter box.

Venom *n* The ink of scorn.

Verbal *adj* Audible, guttural, overstated.

Vice *n* An activity so popular that most civilized societies will elect a president of it.

NORM ALIES

Victimless crime A crime of which there is no victim to speak of, as a crime against the state or character assassination.

DUNCAN DEAUNUTZ

Video *n* A nightmare set to noise. Players wear dark glasses or capped teeth, so as not to confuse the regular hallucinations of viewers.

Visigoth *n* A contemporary of a Hun, or other vandal. An ancient order of noisy barbarians peculiar for its addiction to viewing, or being viewed. Modern barbarians are called **Audio-Visigoths.**

Voodoo *n* A non-Californian cult that produces superstition, trances, and zombies without the aid of the three major networks.

W

Wait *vi* To get what's coming to you.

Walking *n* A kind of low-tech gawkery, of buypeds, restricted to maulls, flea markets, terminals to Las Vegas, cardiac wards, and similar treadmills. Recommended as healthful by physicians and other pettijoggers. According to Prof. Phlattphut, walking was also done, prior to the Human Rights era, on streets.

PERRY PITETTIK

War machine A collective term describing the ordnance of Detente, ranging from simple psychological intimidators such as napalm and mustard gas to the hideously decisive TV bomb, deployed by all seven adversaries and twenty-six media services involved in a standard conflict. TV bombs come in three ghastly calibers:

16mm—equal to 60,000 TNT (Teevee News Tricks)
35mm— " " 100,000 "

And the juggernaut

70mm panabomb—equal to 1,000,000,000 TNTs, with satellites, tapes, replays, monitors, makeups, and shots of terrorists brandishing Go Home CIA letterpressed placards.

TV bomb attacks are said to occur usually from 7 to 9 A.M., at noon, and at 6 and 11 P.M., with three- to five-minute sorties on the hour. The day after a TV bomb attack, horribly disfigured victims can be seen puking and wandering aimlessly in devastated shopmalls in search of aspirins, amphetamines, APC's, and VCR's in a vain attempt to neutralize the debilitating effects of the blasts.

GENERAL HEIPE

Water shortage   A precarious situation, especially in America, where, according to Prof. Divide, the problem is so critical that, in order to conserve the precious fluid, two persons are known to shower together. In California, sometimes three or four (unauthenticated).

JEAUX DOAX

Well-adjusted   Abnormally greedy. See **Adjusted.**

Whale *n*   A large mythical fish, especially white, symbolizing man's eternal struggle to overcome his fear of poaching. The most intelligent ingredient of shoe polish.

Wheat germ *n*   A germ causing those who contract it a loathsome addiction to the munching of weeds, tubers, thistles, alfalfa sprouts, and other fibrosities and infernal inedibles.

THE GALAPAGOS GOURMET

A newly ruminant bovinarian
Caught by the villainous Germ of Wheat!
A former staunch Carnerian
And savorer of medium-rare cuts of meat;
But now consigned up to his adenoids
In brewer's yeast and flavinoids.
What purge of cuds, what cure is forthcoming?
Why, a "script" of hell's chili well worth the cumin!

ROSE HIPZ

White bread *n*   One of the nutritional evils that have caused the average life expectancy to double in the last forty years. *Syn* sugar, salt.

MINNIE STRONEY

Whore *n*   A teaspoonful of vinegar possessing the ability to attract more flies than a barrelful of honey.

Wilderness *n*   Virgin slums.

Wit *n*   A sentimentality called sarcasm by an ignorant fool, and flippancy by a learned one.

Witch doctor   A witch having acquired a taste for beachfront condos, Nikons, and triple-black Cadillacs.

Women *n*   A minority group whose entitlements to war, graft, credit fraud, assassination, shystering, and quackery were, until 1977, traditionally abridged.

HELEN GIRLIE GIGGLY

World-class *adj* 1/9 solar-class. Infinitely inept.

World Series *n* An event restricted to North America.

Writing *n* The ability of an opposed thumb, maligned by thought.

X

X ray *n* A photograph of a bonehead, showing the exact position of an assassin's bullet or a friend's knife.

y

Yak *n* An animal capable of imitating human conversation.

Yam An affirmative declarative in the parlance of the uncivil Mumblolians, residing north of the Rio Grande.

Yellow journalism The only kind.

Yogi *n* A mystic. One of great and holy concentrations, capable of completely controlling the heart rate, blood pressure, respirations, and cash flow of his adherents. In the East the sacred and prescribed postures lead to nirvana; in the West to Rollsroycia.

CALIPH ORNYA

Yusless Young Upwardly-Seeking Loquacious and Enterprising Singles of Suburbia. A network of Perrier derriers.

Z

Zapper *n* *(Zapis ludicrass)* A video device that senses and automatically intercepts only the tasteless and boring segments of prime-time teevee, leaving the astute Test Patterns and Farm Reports for the discriminating viewer.

MIKE ROWPROSESSUR

Zoomorphic *adj* Pertaining to certain silly aboriginal deities in the form of animals—such as the humpback whale—as opposed to our civilized God, the Greenback.

Zoophobia *n* Fear of tourists or snapshooters.

Zooplasty *n* The science of grafting tissue from a higher animal onto a human.

Zucchini *n* A disgusting pulp of the okra, or artichoke, family. Sometimes mistaken for food. A cockroach will eat it only if it is disguised as a tomato or a cheese.

CHEF ROBBERE

Zymurgy *n* (Norse *zymurgla*) The highest attainment of a chemist in his profession, rewarded, through the ages, in every land, by consignment of the chemist's soul to a valhalla, or heaven, and an up-close-and-personal greeting by the supreme spirit. In the original Norse, heaven, for the chemist, was called Brewhalla; the Hindu being Bramahalla; the German, Beerhalla; and the Irish, Brawlhalla.

ST. OTHERWISE